HOW T
Stories and N

by

Fay Goldie

Published by

Malvern Publishing Company Limited
P.O. Box 16
Malvern
Worcestershire
WR14 1UH
England

Hard Back ISBN No. 0-947993-36-3
Paperback ISBN No. 0-947993-38-X

PROLOGUE

That grand man of letters, J.B. Priestley, said shortly before his death at the age of 90, near the end of 1984,

'Being a professional writer means sitting down and writing, every day without fail, however little one feels like it. Just as a banker or a baker has to do his monotonous job every day without making a fuss about it, so writers have to - write.

'But there's something one soon learns - that if one tackles the job, keeps at it, quite soon, in half-an-hour or so, the work takes over and one begins to enjoy it. One's carried along, over the initial apathy or resentment or mental block, and one writes, gathering momentum and enthusiasm in quite a wonderful way. One just writes!'

Jack Priestley did just that all his life to the very end.

And the much loved, hard-working man who has left us so many good plays, novels, and collections of essentially sensible and uniquely inspiring essays and broadcasts, ended with his favourite quotation:

'WE LIVE BY ADMIRATION, HOPE AND LOVE.' And then, he repeated, reflectively, *'ESPECIALLY - LOVE.'*

* * * * *

Other books by the same author include:

Published under the name Fay King:

MEN WITHOUT TRIBES
FRIENDS OF THE BUSHVELD
RED REFLECTIONS
A PRACTICAL GUIDE TO FILM CAREERS
DIAMONDS IN SPRINGBOK VALLEY
BUSHVELD ADVENTURE
BEHIND THE ENEMY'S LINES
THE LOST CITY
THE ZOO MYSTERY
ISLAND OF HAPPY EXILES
FANYANA THE BRAVE
AN EAR OF WHEAT
THE STARS AT HOME

Published under the name Fay Goldie:
LOST CITY OF THE KALAHARI
THE GOLDEN BIRD
ZULU BOY
OSTRICH COUNTRY
RIVER OF GOLD
SUCCESSFUL FREELANCE JOURNALISM

TO BECOME A WRITER ONE MUST THINK A LOT, READ A LOT, AND WRITE EVERY DAY -

AND THEN REVISE WHAT ONE HAS WRITTEN

* * * * *

CONTENTS

CHAPTER ONE

MAKING A START

CHAPTER TWO

WHAT IS A SHORT STORY?

CHAPTER THREE

PLOTS AND TIMING

CHAPTER FOUR

CHARACTERISATION

CHAPTER FIVE

TEMPO, AND DESCRIPTIVE WRITING

CHAPTER SIX

TITLES, DIALOGUES AND DIALECT

CHAPTER SEVEN

METHODS OF WRITING EMOTIONAL SCENES.

CHAPTER EIGHT

WRITING A NOVEL

CHAPTER NINE

AND SO TO WORK

CHAPTER ONE

MAKING A START

Let's get right down to the business of writing short stories and novels, because that's what this book is all about.

What I am offering you are some practical guidelines and suggestions, which I've learnt in the hard school of experience. I do hope they will help you. There isn't space in this book for more, but if it sets you off on the right road to literary fulfilment, it will have achieved what I'm aiming at. I can't ask for more.

You see, ultimately each of us has to learn the craft of writing in our own way, by endlessly thinking, reading, analysing what we've read, observing and listening. And by writing - writing - writing. And then tirelessly revising what we have written.

In spite of what some dreamers think, writing isn't by any means a glamorous or an easy profession or pastime. Nobody with any experience would believe that it is. There is really no other way to become a successful writer than by sheer dedication and hard work.

In spite of which I can assure you that it offers more glittering prizes than one can dream of. And I don't necessarily mean wealth or fame, which certainly don't crown every writer's years of toil.

I mean the prizes of fulfilment and satisfaction, and the excitement that self-expression can bring. I mean the fact that anyone can write who has the mind and the will to do so. And that means whether one lives in a city or the country; in poverty, inwealth, or just scraping by; whatever one's race or creed; whether one has travelled widely or been stuck on one small plot of familiar earth all one's life; whether one has good health or physical handicap; the advantage of a good education, or hardly any. None of these things have much relevance, and should certainly never be used as an excuse for not writing.

It's important to throw overboard any of the boring old excuses for not developing one's writing talents, that one hears ad nauseam from those who are too lazy or too timid to apply themselves to the job, and fight their way through setbacks.

If you can read and you can write, and the burning desire to write is there - that's really all that matters, of that I can assure you.

If you doubt this, I advise you to read the life stories of other writers, past and present, and see how they made it to the top. What did they start out with that you haven't got? Their life stories should inspire you and dispel any self-doubts or excuses.

For instance, when novelist Ursula Bloom died near the end of 1984, at the age of 91, she had 560 books to her credit. Her first book was published when she was only 7, and for many years she produced at least 10 books a year, many under various pen-names.

For years I enjoyed a close and inspiring correspondence with her. She was unfailingly modest and encouraging. Her books ranged from best-selling novels such as *'Perchance to Dream'* to historical novels and autoboigraphies.

Tragedy dogged her life. She endured more than 45 operations for a bone disease contracted in childhood, but nothing daunted her. Her spirit and her achievements remain a source of inspiration to many.

I assume that you're an inexperienced writer, and you want to know how to get those stories that are in your head, down on paper, and then sold to editors so that they will earn you hard cash and, possibly, recognition.

Right?

If you have already tried to write short stories and failed, forget it and try again. You probably only needed to be shown the ropes and given a little recognition in the first place.

Success in writing depends on more than being a born story-teller, although naturally that helps a great deal. One has to understand the tools of the trade and how to use them. And the rules of the game as well.

GET STARTED - NOW

One of the many good things about writing is that you can begin your career here and now. For all you need to make a start are a ball point pen and a notebook. It's as simple as that.

I advise you to start off with several notebooks with spinal binding, small enough to slip into your pocket or handbag. A large students' notebook should always be beside your bed, with a pen. These books open flat, and the pages tear out and are punched for easy filing.

Unless you jot down at once the bright ideas, the twists of plot, the striking titles, the scraps of characterisation which you observe or that flash into your mind, and the gems of dialogue you overhear as you go about your daily affairs, you'll almost certainly lose them.

Don't rely on your memory, however good it may be. Get whatever comes your way *down on paper at the time, if you think it may be of future use to you.*

You may feel self conscious about jotting things down at all sorts of odd moments. But believe me that most successful writers do it as a matter of course.

Few present day writers have won themselves more spectacular literary success among fiction-millionaires than novelist Jeffrey Archer.

In record time he became one of the three fastest-selling paperback authors in Britain - others are John le Carre and Frederick Forsythe - and if you're not familiar with the work of these three short story writers and novelists, I hope you soon will be. They can teach us so much.

Well, not long ago Jeffrey Archer was met at Carlisle station by a journalist sent to interview him. As the crowd of alighting passengers cleared, Jeffrey Archer's solitary figure could be seen down on one knee at the far end of the platform, his suitcase serving as a desk, scribbling away furiously.

'Mr Archer, what on earth are you doing?' the reporter asked anxiously.

'Terribly sorry,' Archer said, still scribbling and without looking up. 'I've got to get this down...'

Now if this man, still in his forties and at the peak of his literary fame, could learn such tricks to help himself swing across the abyss of bankruptcy and an abandoned political career by his single-minded determination to write good yarns that sell in their millions - well, you have to take note, don't you? Especially if you too want to succeed. Which you can, if you really want to. And that's fact, not fiction.

The point I want to impress on you is that Jeffrey Archer, like le Carre, Forsyth, Beryl Bainbridge, and most other successful writers, is a 'jotter.' Notebooks are always within easy reach day and night, and they don't rely on memory. Experience has taught them better.

Bag those precious butterflies that hover round you, innocently released by your kids, your neighbours, fellow shoppers or work colleagues. Don't just stand there and let them fly away forever, and then complain that you haven't an idea in your head to work on.

BOOKS YOU'LL NEED

After you've hired, borrowed, or preferably bought a typewriter, which is a necessity, and the supply of ball-point pens and notebooks I've mentioned, there are a few books of reference that you simply can't do without.

Your first purchase should be a good Classical Dictionary with bold type, for you'll be referring to it at all hours of the day and night

Words are the most important tools a writer has and they must be *used* , just as an artist uses paints and a musician musical instruments.

No matter what the standard of your education may have been, you will certainly be studying words, and how best to use them, all your writing life. So begin now, and keep it up.

You'll need a good Encyclopaedia, or similar book of wide reference.

Another book all writers must h've for frequent reference is *'The Writers' and Artists' Yearbook..'* It isn't expensive, and it will be money well spent. Keep up to date with editors' and publishers' requirements by investing in a current paper back edition every year or so.

In this book you will find the names, addresses and requirements of magazines and book publishers throughout most of the English-speaking world. You can't hope to manage without it.

There is also a wealth of information concerning the presentation of manuscripts, and how to submit your work to editors, and chapters dealing with copyright, income tax on literary earnings, literary agents, writing for radio and television, and much more. As far as I know it is the only book of its kind in print, and it's invaluable to any writer.

Don't just buy it. Study it closely and refer to it frequently. It is utterly reliable.

And one more 'must' - *'Roget's Thesaurus'*, or to give it its full title, *'The Everyday Roget's Thesaurus of Synonyms and Antonyms'*. You can buy this treasure of a book in paperback, which is easier to carry around with you. If it's new to you, it will be a revelation - and a friend.

BE PROFESSIONAL

Always be sure your work looks professional when it goes out. It must be easy to read, correctly and attractively laid out, and the spelling, grammer and punctuation should be carefully checked. And checked again.

From the first you'll be competing with experienced professionals, but don't let that daunt you. Accept it as a challenge, for that's what it is.

Although, as I've said, you can find out in *'The Writer's and Artist's Yearbook'* all you need to know about preparing and submitting manuscripts, as well as correcting proofs, let me explain how you should check the number of words in a manuscript, whether it be that of a short story or a book.

If your manuscript is short, say no more than about 3,000 words, then you must count the exact number of words, and state it on the front cover sheet of your MS. This is important, for editors and publishers need this information. Editors must restrict the length of their stories to the available space in their publications to be filled, and publishers must have a good idea of the length of a book for print reasons.

For MSS longer than, say, 3000 words, count the exact number of words on each of five typed pages, chosen at random. Add them together, divide the total by five, and there you have the approximate number of words to an average page. You then multiply the number of words on this 'Average page' by the number of pages in your MS - and hey presto! there you have the approximate number of words of your complete typescript.

It may be stating the obvious, but the reason why the five pages of manuscript must be chosen at random is because pages with short paragraphs or a great deal of dialogue will have fewer words than pages of solid, long paragraphs.

* * * * *

An author is often asked to cut the length of a manuscript, or lengthen it, to fit the requirements of an editor or publisher.

Never show 'temperament' when you receive such requests. Just get on with the job, and see how much you can learn from doing it.

And don't just 'pad' it out to the required length. Give a great deal of thought and care to every word you cut out or add.

* * * * *

LITERARY AGENTS

No writer's job begins and ends with writing a story or a novel. Still less with simply dreaming of 'one day' writing a best-seller that will shake the world and bring you a fortune.

A story must be thought about, visualised and felt.

It must be written down.

It must then be revised.

And the final typescript, with a carbon copy, must be produced.

Then checked again, and again, for possible mistakes.

Almost all successful writers go over their work two or three times, or more, to make sure it reads smoothly, and that there are no glaring factual, typing or spelling errors. This polishing may be tedious, but it simply must be done.

If I may quote from Jeffrey Archer once more - after all, he attained best-seller status with his first novel, and with every subsequent book.

'It takes me two years to think about and research a book,' he said recently. 'I then get down to the agonising work of writing the first draft, always by hand. Then come ruthless corrections. And another complete draft. Altogether I write 11 or 12 drafts before I'm satisfied, and the thing's typed, then corrected, and sent to my Agent. (Debbie Owen, wife of Dr. David Owen, who is a Literary Agent.) I actually re-wrote the latest book, which I've just handed over, 13 times before I was finally satisfied with it.'

When your MS is finally ready to go out, it must be submitted for sale. This isn't easy. Don't imagine that a literary agent, acting as Fairy Godmother to your brain children, will do this for you from your first book or story.

Unless your work shows most unusual promise, or you have a good literary agent in the family, you will have to convince an agent that it will sell and that the public and editors will like it, before an agent will agree to handle your work for you.

After all, Literary Agents are only paid *ON RESULTS*, so it isn't likely that an agent will take on the work of marketing the manuscripts of untried, amateur writers, the expense involved in time and postage makes this prohibitive.

Literary agents are, in the main, only concerned with the marketing of books or serials. Short stories must be the work of established writers before they will interest literary agents.

As I've said before, study your *'Writers' and Artists' Yearbook'*, which will tell you all you need to know about direct marketing or using a Literary Agent.

So you will have to study possible markets for your stories, and tailor your work for them. There's no sense at all in writing 'misfits' that stand little or no hope of fitting the needs, in style and length, of the magazines you have in mind.

In this tough, challenging field, common sense and hard work are as necessary as inborn talent. And that's up to you, isn't it?

It's important that we understand all we can about the construction of short stories. So we'll go on now to analysing the various types of story, and learning as much as possible about plot construction, characterisation, writing dialogue, descriptive writing, handling - and feeling - emotional scenes, and how to deal with the very tricky time factor in our work.

* * * * *

CHAPTER TWO

WHAT IS A SHORT STORY?

If you were to ask a dozen successful short story writers that question, you'd probably get twelve different answers.

Because, of course, there are all kinds of short story, including the hard-pressed action story, the fantasy, love story, science-fiction, crime, and what are called purely literary stories, which are little more than exquisitely observed fragments of life, with hardly any plot and very little action.

But I think all would agree that a short story should interest and entertain the reader, first and foremost. Those are basic requirements of every type of story.

To begin with, a short story is *NOT* a short novel. Nor is it a sketch.

You see, a novel may carry its action through several years, or even several generations. It may feature only a few characters, or hundreds of characters. It may deal with any number of incidents and emotional crises, and the action may range over half the world.

There's elbow room in a novel. A writer can really spread himself and give his imagination wings.

The short story must be strictly limited in time and action, and in the number of its characters. It should have a single emotion or mood.

Nor is the short story a sketch, because a sketch is literally an outline, covering no more than slight character studies and incidents. The short story is much more than outline - it is a complete picture, however short it may be.

In other words - one thing, happening to one central person, and creating in the mind of the reader one emotion. Very roughly, that is a short story.

Let's break it down, and study it, shall we?

The short story plot is concerned with one event or emotional crisis complete in itself. No series of events of equal importance can be accurately described as a short story.

When I said that a short story must concern one person, I meant that the plot usually shows events in their relation to one character - the key character. There are usually other characters, of course, who have a certain importance, but it is this one main character's share in the reaction to the events in the story that really matters.

And the phrase, 'creating in the reader one emotion'...

There is no time in the span of the short story to run through a whole range of emotions. The author must strike and hold one emotional note. It may be humour, tension, romance, nostalgia, horror, pathos, adventure, frustration or compassion. But only one of these must predominate from first to last.

FIRST, SECOND, OR THIRD PERSON?

There are several distinct ways of telling a story. You may find that one or other comes more naturally, more easily, to you than others, or is best suited to a particular story.

You can write in the First Person, as though telling the story as a personal experience.

Here's Laurie Lee's introduction to his story, *'The Opposite Sex'*:

'It wasn't the discovery of sex that affected my life so much as the first occasion that I met it head on.'

Most of this enchanting author's work is written in the first person, from his wealth of experience. Remember his novel, *'Cider with Rosie'?* It's a classic of this kind of writing.

Of course you could use variations of the first-person narrative, such as a diary or letters, although neither is very popular at the moment.

The most acceptable method of telling a story today is in the Third Person. Let your characters do all the work. Let them explain through their actions, reactions and dialogue, how they are working out their problems.

WHAT EDITORS WANT

The editor of a leading American magazine said with feeling when asked what kind of stories he wanted:

'They must move me. Make me laugh or make me cry. But they *must* move me!'

Let me suggest the kind of stories most editors appear to be looking for at the moment, if what they say and what they print is an accurate guide:

They want stories about lonely people looking for love, security, or just a purpose for living, and preferably finding it.

They want stories about the terrible - or funny - confusion of adolescence, and about how these young people grow into adults.

You may remember the 'angry young men' of the sixties, who disturbed the western world's reading, theatre and screen. If that traumatic experience was long before your time, you may well have heard about it, or come across it in your reading.

Well, a publisher told me recently that he's receiving a flood of MSS, some very promising indeed, written by today's dissollusioned youngsters, many unemployed, many bitter or afraid of the threat of The Big Bang which could end the world we all live in.

I just hope with all my heart that their flame won't be blown out by the cold breath belched by yesterday's angry youth, many of whom are now sitting pretty at the top of the pile, before some at least have had their say printed between the covers of books and magazines.

...I believe readers and editors want stories where tenderness and compassion triumph over cynicism, and where true charity moves mean, small people toward good.

Most people really do want a cheerful read with plenty of heart. And I *don't* mean slush. Heart! And Hope.

Editors want action stories that will grip readers and hold them enthralled from first to last.

They want strong escapist yarns.

They want wild life stories; stories about mans' struggle with or against the elements - drought, flood, famine, pestilence, fire, earthquake, wild seas, or becalmed ships.

They want humour. Oh, indeed they want humour! All the good racey humour they can get.

And that's just the beginning of it. The range is as wide and deep as life itself.

THREE MAIN GROUPS

Let's break down the different categories of short story into three main groups for analysis.

There's the Short-Short Story. The Magazine Story And the Literary Story

Short-short stories are used in week-end magazine sections of some national newspapers, as well as in certain magazines.

I'm reminded of the experience of William Saroyan, that master of the short-short story in America, who was actually starving in a single room when he created a market for his kind of stories in the daily edition of The Saturday Evening Post.

He bombarded the editor with a story a day, delivering them himself because he couldn't afford the postage. He told the editor that he'd continue to offer him a story every day until he realised that his magazine couldn't afford to refuse them.

It took some time to break down the editor's resistance because the stories were quite unlike anything he'd ever published. But eventually Saroyan got through to the Editor, and those short-short stories of his, which ran to more than 1,000 words, and were brilliantly funny, appeared every day for years, hoisting the unknown young Armenian/American writer to the top of the literary ladder, and changing the policy of America's most prestigious and top-paying magazine.

That's what it means to have complete faith in one's work, and to refuse to accept defeat.

O'Henry was another brilliant writer of unique short-short stories, who began by writing his stories on scraps of paper while sitting on park benches in New York, homeless and penniless. His stories, too, made literary history.

If you're unfamiliar with the stories of Saroyan and O'Henry, I strongly advise you to read them again and again until they become part of your memory bank. They're masterpieces of their kind.

Don't imagine that you can succeed as a short story writer if you haven't studied the work of contemporary and past writers.

You simply must read a lot, think a lot, and write a lot. You can't hope to succeed unless you do.

* * * * *

THE SHORT-SHORT STORY

The length of the short-short story is usually between 1,000 and 2,000 words, with the most popular lengths 1,200 to 1,500 words.

In this matter of length you must be rigid with yourself. If the editor stipulates 1,250 words, then your stories should run to exactly that length, because that's the space they're meant to fill. No more, no less.

One of the many joys of writing these very short stories is that nearly all the work can be done in your head before writing or typing them down. They can be an ideal mental occupation to work on while gardening, commuting, standing about in queues or lying awake at night.

Another point in their favour, as far as the writer is concerned, is the knowledge that while a long story is usually skimmed through by the reader, the short-short story is savoured. You might say that it's often lip-read, with every word important.

You can learn more writing discipline from this type of work, probably, than any other. Action, dialogue, description, all have to be compressed, with nothing allowed that doesn't actively help to further the action or draw in characters and background. They're gems you can polish and delight in.

Just listen to these examples taken from short-short stories:

'He opened the door to find that snow and cold had conspired with the day-long wind to make departure impossible."

Not a word that could be cut without definite loss. So much for the short-short story, but a magazine story could have been expressed like this:

'It was snowing hard. The wind had been blowing for hours, and the temperature must have dropped to zero. He opened the door, then shut it quickly, staring out through the frosted glass. He could never get through until the storm had blown itself out.'

Which is about twice the number of words, and says nothing more.

Characterisation should be cut to the bare bones in your short-short stories. As in this extract from an American 'Redbook' story.

'Across the table in the nightclub where Barbara had produced this long-touted brother of hers, Ann had thought he looked as though he could do anything - tall, slim, no hips, dark crew cut, laugh wrinkles.' The characters and the scene come through.

When you're writing dialogue for these very short stories, bear in mind who is talking. Let their conversation reveal characters for what they are and what they're doing.

Get inside the very skin of your characters; participate in the action; listen with your inner writer's ear to the dialogue. Remember the difference between compressed writing, and stilted writing. The difference, of course, is rhythm.

Just because these brief stories are written so quickly, don't clutch an idea, slap it down on paper, and send it out to the first likely editor who comes to mind.

They need thought, personal identification, revision, and they must be written for a specific market.

* * * * *

The Magazine Story is just what its name implies. It refers to that wide range of short fiction written for the weekly and monthly magazines, which abound, and which are read by millions of people, particularly women these days, although mens' magazines were very popular some years ago.

Probably most of your stories will be written for magazines of one kind or another. They cover a very wide field, so it is of first importance that you study them, and learn from close study just what each editor is looking for.

A sure guide to the kind of stories that will come most easily to you, is to write for your own favourite magazine.

Every editor has in mind a very clear idea of the kind of reader he or she is catering for - it's no hit and miss affair. Every member of the editorial staff of a magazine could describe the reader they have in mind throughout the planning of each issue, which dictates the kind of stories they buy, the way those stories are illustrated and presented, and the marketing of the magazine.

The advertisements the magazine attracts must be directed at this imaginary reader. Everything, the style, the appearance from the cover through the fiction, features, and regular editorial articles, is planned for this reader's specific interest.

So, to begin with, I suggest that you choose your favourite magazine, or magazines, and go ahead to study it in depth, making notes as you go along.

One issue will tell you a little, but not enough. You must study consecutive issues of that magazine over a period. Note the number of stories appearing in every issue; the length; the kind of people and situations that make up these stories.

The illustrations will help to give you a good idea of the reader the editor has in mind. Young, bright, romantic, or independent? You must know her if you're going to write for her.

Just ask yourself - Is there a day in my life when I'm not moved by the dramas being played around me by family, friends, or strangers whose lives touch mine?

I don't believe there could be such a day. Unless one is fossilised, that is, or has withdrawn from active human participation in everyday life. Life is only humdrum and without drama if one deliberately prefers it that way. I'm sure every one of us, when we open ourselves to life, experiences something of the pain and the joy, the humour, sorrow, and the revelation of life. The constant Human Experience.

Very well, then - we must write about it. We must choose our characters, set them in challenging situations, and weave action about them.

Every part of it can excite and challenge you; choosing your title, the names, appearances and peculiarities of the people you create. Writing dialogue can be fascinating, and ending at exactly the right moment for maximum impact. It will demand your best thought and writing.

Learn all you can from life. Don't draw back from it. It isn't what happens to us that matters. It's our reaction to experience that's so important to us as individuals, and as writers.

If you're stuck in a dull, undemanding, uncongenial job, get out of it! Do something different that gets you among people that will excite, teach and draw you out of your shell. It's by watching and listening to stimulating people that you'll find your story material.

LITERARY STORIES

The markets for literary stories are often to be found in anthologies published periodically by certain publishers, in so-called 'literary magazines', and in collections of your own 'serious' stories when you've written enough to compile into a book.

If we're going to write serious magazine and literary stories, we must think deeply about everything in life that touches us.

Let's take loneliness, for instance. Let's think about it and see what we can learn from it.

Sooner or later every one of us is faced with the fact that we're alone in the world, responsible for our own lives. The realisation comes in various ways, but it certainly does come and must be coped with.

The way we handle this often shattering knowledge of our essential aloneness is the vitally important thing. The fortunate ones leap from the cold hard rock on which they've landed, straight into some kind of reassuring spiritual awareness. They learn that the frightening consciousness of mental or physical isolation is often used to teach us that, spiritually, man is never alone.

Sometimes our most bitter moments of loss awaken us to the golden understanding of the spiritual oneness of all mankind.

This subject of loneliness, which affects us all in some measure, offers endless aspects upon which short stories and novels can be built.

Most people search for Love, Security and Fulfilment. Those three things. *HOW* people do it, by opening their lives to love, or by retreating into strange little worlds of fantasy of their own, is material for countless stories.

Writers should understand loneliness more easily than most people, because writing is essentially a solitary occupation.

Dig down into this word and learn all you can about it. Find out what it can do to a person's spirit, mind and body. It will teach you a great deal about your fellow man - and about yourself.

Try to comprehend the loneliness of an old person faced with blindness. The abandoned child. The soldier in battle, or the person awaiting a major operation. The crippled dancer. The ship-wrecked. The mother whose child dies at birth.

Of course it isn't a cheerful subject. It's sad or tragic. But the serious writer must face truths. The more deeply we study life, the wider our horizon of understanding. And the more there will be to write about.

THE PLOTLESS STORY

Literary stories don't always have to rely on a plot. They may be no more than a view through a window - looking out, or looking in; a short, concentrated view of life.

Although it may look deceptively easy, believe me it isn't. It calls for much skill. And, watch yourself, you may be using it as an escape shoot to take you out of the difficult exercise of plotting your stories.

There are, then, three distinct categories of the short story. The Short-short story. The Magazine Story. And the Literary Story.

Study these stories, analyse them, understand their markets. And start writing the kind of story that most appeals to you - as a reader and a writer.

JOT IT DOWN

Begin *now* to jot things down in your notebooks, and open files for your cuttings of interesting material, if you haven't made a start already. Ideas, characters, titles or plots, the description of some place, incident, animal or tree; intriguing news items, or conversation. Get it all down for future use.

LOOK ABOUT YOU. What kind of day is it today? Describe it in as few words as possible so that you convey the feel, appearance, sound and mood of this moment. Being a writer means that you must be 'tuned in' twenty-four hours a day.

If you find that sleep eludes you and you're quite alone in the dark ship of night, don't fret or panic or reach for that sleeping tablet. Make the most of it. Enjoy it. Relax and respond to the magic of it. Watch the shadows, the dawn of a new day or the coming up of the moon. Listen to the remarkable variety of sounds peculiar to the night. The wind in the trees outside your bedroom window, or the night traffic in the street below; the owls and cats and brittle insect sounds. And, if you're lucky enough to be wide awake when the dawn chorus really heralds the morning, listen - and describe it in words. Reach for your bedside jotter and get it down even if there's insufficient light for you to read your words.

Make the most of every waking minute and make it part of your celebration. No matter if today brings you pain or anxiety, frustration or sorrow, you can find cause for celebration - if you look for it. You're alive, aren't you? You want to develop whatever talents you were born with, and become a writer, don't you? Well, now is the time to work at it. With so much going on all about you, filling your eyes and ears, your nostrils and skin. How does that sunshine, that rain or snow or wind, feel as it whispers or rushes past you, as it wets your lips or as snowflakes come to rest on your eyelashes, gentle as apricot petals? *This* moment, *this* day, *this* year of your life are unique, for you to record in words.

Store all the sights, sounds and emotions of this moment in the bank of your memory. You can be certain that, one day, you will gladly rediscover them when you're working on a story or a novel, and life will be breathed into your words. Be quite sure that nothing is ever wasted, if you're a writer. Everything will come into its own in time.

MAKE A START NOW

This is what I earnestly advise you to do:

1. Think about a character until he or she comes alive in your mind. Watch and listen to them for a while. Then describe that person in a few words. Don't smother them with words. Get them down on the page in a few words. A sharp, clear outline. Then cut this down to fewer words still.

2. Build up the environment surrounding your character. Think about it until you, too, are living in it. Describe it briefly, choosing your words carefully and truthfully.

3. Face your character with the kind of problem life would probably produce for him - or her. God knows there's variety enough. Describe it.

4. In your mind's eye, watch your character react to that problem in their own characteristic way. Write it down.

And there you have the basic material for a story, haven't you? You have the character or characters, the problem facing them, and you know they must find a solution. You can see how important it is that you know your characters intimately, the way they will think and react and solve their problems. Fun, isn't it?

Right. Get started. You want to be a successful writer, and you can be one. But only if you write. Only if you observe, read, think, study, and use your God-given imagination.

Think - and write!

* * * * *

For five rewarding years I ran The New Era School of Writing, single-handed. I gave it everything I had to give, and it was the most worth while work I have ever done.

Hundreds of would-be writers, some with little more than a dream or a desire to write, others variously talented, most of them quite untried, passed through my school. Those who stuck out the hard pace I set - who were about 95% of those who enrolled - developed into successful writers in almost every literary field.

They became short story writers, novelists, journalists, photo-journalists, writers of childrens' books and educational textbooks, columnists, radio and television writers - the whole spectrum! I am still dazzled and delighted by their continued success in the fields of work they chose, and, I believe, so are many of them.

WISHFUL WRITERS

I mention this to convince you that I do know what I'm saying when I keep hammering away at the importance of making a start - now!

Most of those men and women had been wishful writers for years. Tomorrow was the time to begin their writing careers. It never came. It never does if ones' wishbone is where ones' backbone ought to be.

TODAY IS THE DAY!

I simply insisted that *TODAY IS THE DAY!* That one must have the courage to take the plunge - at once. And the results were dramatically successful. They were beyond my wildest dreams, and in many cases, beyond theirs.

So I say to you, begin now! Start to work on a short story right away. It may be the first you've ever tried your hand at. Which is all the more reason why you should tackle it at once, without any more shilly-shallying.

All right, it may not be a masterpiece. It may not sell right away. That's not the point. You will have begun your writing career. Broken the ice. That's what matters.

I once knew a man who had played around with the idea of being a writer for eighteen years. He described himself as a writer to people who wouldn't be likely to check up on his boast. He even went so far as to write the word 'Writer' on his Passport, where he should have written 'Clerk'. He lived a fantasy, and felt wretched.

Then he found the courage to put words down on paper. To try himself out. He did it secretly because he was so afraid of failure, and of 'looking ridiculous', as he confessed.

Two years later his first book was published. It was a runaway success and it changed his life. What I found hard to swallow was the fact that, instead of being overjoyed by his success, he used to whine about the years he'd wasted dithering on the brink instead of diving in and proving his talent. He had only himself to blame for his delayed fame and fortune. A fact I wasn't backward in pointing out. Surely we should celebrate success when it comes our way, with a thankful heart, remembering those who never achieve it.

THE FAMILY OF WRITERS

In our next chapter we're going to study plot-construction, and how to handle the Time Factor. They're both vitally important for the short story writer, or the novelist.

I want you to feel that you're part of the great family of writers, here and now. Read about fellow writers - how they work, the hurdles they have to take in their stride. Read their books, especially the autobiographies. You must keep up to date with published work, world-wide.

Remember that we're all struggling forward together. No matter where you may live, however isolated you may feel at times, you're not really alone. Other men and women are writing their hearts out in every country, every province, every town and village. I often feel writing is the most universal activity there is - after love-making. Oh no, you're not alone my friend. You aren't the only person who has received yet another rejection from an editor or publisher today. You aren't alone in dreaming of success as a writer, and of working towards that shining star. We're all struggling forward together. There's comfort in the knowledge.

Do try to let me help you, through this book, to realise your ambition to write stories and novels that will sell. You must have that ambition or you wouldn't be reading this book, would you?

Is it a deal, fellow writer?

Fine! Let's go.

* * * * *

CHAPTER THREE

PLOTS and TIMING

In this chapter we're going to study the structure of the short story, and then we'll go on to study Timing, which can so easily spell success or failure for a writer.

One of the ways in which I like to think of the short story is to liken it to a house. The action of a short story will probably take place in no more than one room of the house - the bedroom, kitchen, living-room or the study. The choice is yours.

The whole exercise must be compact, carefully laid out and decorated, not over-crowded, unless a tight family scene or a poverty trap is in the background.

If you were working on a novel, you see, your characters would no doubt make good use of every room in the building, as well as spreading themselves and their action out into the garden and the street, or much further afield.

For a novel you would need plenty of room for your action, chapter after chapter, as the plot develops, and as other characters come and go.

WHAT IS A PLOT?

You may well be asking, 'What is a plot, anyway?'

Explained as simply as possible - for my sake, not necessarily yours - a plotted story must have a beginning, a middle, and an end. In that order.

And if that sounds obvious to you, believe me it isn't to all inexperienced writers. You'd be surprised how often a story is dragged onto the stage tail first, like a stubborn mule, with the writer giving away the 'surprise end' in the first few paragraphs of the story, so that the whole act, the whole structure, falls flat.

I think it is generally believed by writers who are young at the game that everyone born with the itch to write is also born with a knowledge of plotting.

Nothing could be wider of the truth. There are singularly few natural plot-spinners even among extremely talented writers. Most writers have had to learn to construct plots the hard way, by much thought and by practise.

Until you've accepted that fact, and fully realised that weakness in plot-construction is something that can be overcome by almost everyone, it can cause much self-doubt and depression, not to mention failure in writing stories that will sell.

I assure you from much experience that if you really tackle this job you can master it. Have no doubt about that. You can reach the point where your brain becomes an automatic plotter, and you find it doing the job without pain, and almost without effort. It can be tremendous fun.

That quickened mind of yours will pounce on an idea and begin to develop it. Because every plot begins with an idea. Just as every oak begins with an acorn.

The simple formula which forms the skeleton of your plot must be so mastered by you that it becomes part of your subconscious. Out of it plots will, in time, automatically spring ready-made into your conscious mind.

You may well find that, after much hard work at plot-construction, you'll awake from sleep or from day-dreaming, with an intriguing plot materialising, or fully formed, in your mind, all ready to be clothed in words, polished, and sent out into the world.

If you really persevere, to your delight you'll find plots will be popping up faster than you can get them down on paper - but then you'll have those notebooks handy, won't you? It's largely a matter of learning to recognise them when you see them. And going to work on them as soon as possible, until you've achieved a story that thrills and satisfies you.

One thing is certain in story writing. Work is always involved.

BEWARE OF FANCY FORMULAS

A cry that haunts me is this: 'I'm no earthly good at constructing plots. Surely there are easy formulas one can use?'

It haunts me because I have heard it so often.

Of course, there are dozens and dozens of formulas for plot construction which you can buy. There are automatic plot-finders on the market that make exciting promises. And I've known several desperate would-be story writers who have actually paid fancy prices for them, BUT I'VE NEVER KNOWN ONE TO WORK!

Believe me there is no solution to a weakness in plot-construction - except to accept the fact that very few of us are born plotters, and then for us to get down to the hard work of learning this vital part of the writer's craft.

This I can tell you from personal experience, both as one who agonised and despaired of ever building story skeletons that would stand up on their own two feet while being worked on, and not collapse into meaningless piles of bones. And as a fundamentally lazy creature who for many years firmly believed that day-dreaming and thinking were one and the same thing, which of course they aren't. They're the antithesis of one another. One is self-indulgence, the other constructive work.

If you tackle this job you can master it. Have no doubt about it.

One of the most popular automatic devices for plotting, which has earned a small fortune for the non-writing man who thought it out, comes in the form of a natty little box of printed cards filed in it under headings, card-index fashion.

One section is marked FEMALE CHARACTERS, another MALE CHARACTERS, one SETTINGS, and others come under PROBLEMS, OBSTACLES TO FULFILMENT, COMPLICATIONS, CRISIS and CLIMAX.

They certainly demonstrate what a versatile and complicated creature man is - and the holes he can burrow or fall into.

The idea was to choose a card from each section of the index without peeping to see what you'd got.

Then you read the hand of cards you'd chosen, and worried yourself silly working the oddly assorted characters, locations, problems, complications and crises to somehow fit the improbable climax.

I can think of a hundred easier and cheaper ways of driving yourself insane. But I can't think of a sillier way for a serious writer to set about learning the beautiful, logical architecture of plot-construction.

I believe that it's as essential for the writer to master plot construction, as it is for the artist to have a thorough understanding of pictorial construction. Composition is all-important in any creative work.

* * * * *

A BEGINNING, A MIDDLE, AND AN END.

As I said earlier, every story must have a beginning, a middle, and an end. For the moment please accept that as a fact. We can study the exceptions as we go along, for there are exceptions to most rules in life.

You must begin, in the first paragraph, to draw your reader into the time and place of your story. Your beginning must introduce your reader to the locale - the setting in which the action will take place - and to your key character or characters. It should also drop a hint as to the kind of story about to unfold.

Never muff your opening with wordy descriptions. Snap into action right away. You've got to hold and keep your reader's interest from the word 'Go!'.

Here's an introduction to a short story called *'The Luncheon'*, from Jeffrey Archer's collection, *'A Quiver Full of Arrows':*

'She waved at me across the crowded room of the St. Regis hotel in New York. I waved back realising I knew the face but I was unable to place it. She squeezed past waiters and guests and had reached me before I had a chance to ask anyone who she was.'

Just as all his stories snap into action with the first words, so they all end with a quirky, unexpected flash at the end. They aren't profound, or deeply moving. Just smoothly told, urbanely satiric, very professional stories.

Another example? O.K. Something quite different. 'It was the afternoon of my eighty-first birthday, and I was in bed with my cotomite when Ali announced that the archbishop had come to see me.'

And another master story-teller, George Orwell's opening words to '1984':

'It was a bright, clear day in April and the clocks were striking thirteen...'

Now I want to draw your attention to a book that may help and interest you. Novelist and story-writer, Fay Weldon, has written it, she says, to show new writers the truth of what the professionals say - 'If your opening captures the reader, you've hooked him for good.'

Her book is called *'Letters to Alice'*, and in it she gives an imaginary neice a correspondence course in the craft of writing.

CONFLICT

Having introduced your locale and key character you must now bring conflict into your story. Without it there would be no action. No motive. No story.

There are basically three types of conflict as far as the short story is concerned:

1. Conflict between man and man.
2. Conflict between man and nature.
3. Conflict between man and himself.

I want you to form the habit of analysing stories as you read them. Make notes in the margin as you read. The family will get used to coming across your marginal notes as they read. If you write them in soft pencil they can always be erased should they annoy anyone.

You'll see that every story is about something. That a problem has been presented which the characters must face and grapple with - which results in conflict of one kind or another.

This doesn't necessarily mean physical conflict. Mental conflict between two or more people, or simply within oneself, can be just as vital and rivetting.

So the middle of your story must be concerned with action. With conflict. And it must build up to a climax.

You should know by heart the EIGHT SIGNPOSTS that will direct your story from the beginning to the end. They are, of course:

LOCALE

CHARACTERS

PROBLEM

OBSTACLE TO THE FULFILMENT OF DESIRE

COMPLICATION

PREDICAMENT

CRISIS

CLIMAX

It won't be enough just to memorise those eight signposts. You'll have to do more than that. You must study as many stories as you can - an excellent idea is to read one story - really read it! - every day without fail. Analyse these stories, and jot down the signposts as you recognise them.

Then write a brief outline or synopsis of each story, and pin it to the magazine in which it appeared.

I can't over-emphasise the importance of a healthy plot for your story. Your plot will be too feeble to hold the reader's interest if there is no conflict brought about by a struggle for or about something. And, whatever that 'something' is, it must be important and strong enough to make the struggle worth while.

THE END

Never allow a story to fizzle out. It must end with a gasp, a shudder, a smile, or even a tear. When your reader puts your story down he must feel satisfied. You haven't broken faith and let him down at the end.

As an editor explained the other day, 'The most common fault in the stories submitted to me is a falling-off at the end, a lack of punch. A story should build up all the way through, and then end on a strong note. The action's finished. The characters have carried you along through the action - then it's finished. Not another word should be added. No good play would drop the curtain on an anti-climax. The moment to end must be just right, inevitable.'

I appreciate that when you've worked long and hard on a story, and the end's in sight, the impulse is to bring it to a close, to do a quick revision - then send it out, hopefully to sell.

But you simply mustn't rush it at the end. If you feel suddenly exhausted, played out, and sick to death with the story you've worked on for days, weeks, even months here's what I advise you to do:

Put it away in a drawer for a little while. Turn your mind and your hand to something else. Then, when you come back to it you'll feel a new enthusiasm for it, and you'll be eager to go to work and give it the twist in the tail and the polish it demands.

You'll be wasting your time if you don't.

Bear in mind that ENTHUSIASM is the magic ingredient you must capture in all your work. Without enthusiasm your work will be dull, lack-lustre, without fire or poetry.

FAMOUS 36 DRAMATIC SITUATIONS

Perhaps it will help if I give you *'The Famous 36 Dramatic Situations'* which the French writer, Georges Polti, drafted a very long time ago. They are as fresh and as true today as ever they were, or ever will be.

You see, the importance of sound plot-construction has always been recognised by the masters of fiction as being vital to this art form. Endless thought, discussion and experiment have been devoted to it, and we should appreciate the legacy we have inherited.

Not only did Georges Polti work out the 36 dramatic situations which he declared were the only possible ones a writer could use when constructing his stories. Count Carlo Gozzi , the great Italian dramatist of ther 18th century, made an exactly similar list of 36 basic situations and found that the number couldn't be added to by any amount of thought on the subject.

Both Goethe and Schiller agreed with them, and approved of this list of situations.

Here is the list worked out by Polti and Gozzi:

1. Supplication

2. Deliverance

3. Crime pursued by vengeance

4. Vengeance taken for kindred upon kindred

5. Pursuit

6. Disaster

7. Falling prey to cruelty or misfortune
8. Revolt
9. Daring enterprise
10. Abduction
11. The enigma
12. Obtaining
13. Enmity of kinsmen
14. Rivalry of kinsmen
15. Murderous adultery
16. Madness
17. Fatal imprudence
18. Involuntary crimes of love
19. Slaying of an unrecognised kinsman
20. Self-sacrifice for passion
21. Self-sacrifice for kindred
22. Sacrifice for an ideal
23. Necessary sacrifice for loved ones
24. Rivalry of Inferior and Superior
25. Adultery
26. Crimes of love
27. Discovery of a loved ones' dishonour
28. Obstacles to love
29. An enemy loved

30. Ambition

31. Conflict with a God

32. Mistaken jealousy

33. Mistaken judgement

34. Remorse

35. Recovery of a lost one

36. Loss of a beloved one

When you've studied the list you'll have to agree that in every plot conceived one or more of these situations has formed the basis of the story. The masters of fiction are as sure of this today as they were a few hundred years ago when it was so carefully compiled.

There's a remarkable thing about this list, which may seem arid to you as you look at it now - and that is that there will come a time, if you seriously study short story writing and apply yourself to it, when you have only to glance at any one of these 36 curt statements to have it miraculously blossom in your mind into a full-blown plot. These are dynamic seeds which short story writers have been wise enough to take very seriously indeed over the years. And do so today. See what they can do for YOU...

THE TIME FACTOR

I believe most editors would agree that the most important single ingredient of success for a writer depends on Timing. This implies appreciating the mood of the reading public at a particular moment in history, and catering for it.

Some fortunate writers have a genius for timing. Just as some actors have. It can be an inborn guide, or instinct, but with the vast majority it's something they've acquired through patient study, observation, and sensitivity, and, of course a good measure of common sense.

This is more obvious when longer work is concerned, such as novels and autobiographies. But it certainly applies to short stories as well.

I learnt this lesson thoroughly immediately after World War II.

Those of us who were young writers at the time produced a spate of war stories and books, and we were devastated and very surprised when rejections came thick and fast.

We were writing about what we knew only too well from first hand experience. Our stories dealt with espionage, epic battles, the bombardment of cities, prisoner-of-war camps, broken families due to the stresses of war, or wartime romances.

We'd heard about the importance of Timing. Surely the war was in everyone's mind? It must concern every type of reader to some degree.

Then how was it that editors and publishers didn't want what we were writing from deep personal experience, often from shattered lives?

What we couldn't see at the time was that people were heart-broken, confused, or exhausted by the war. Tired of thinking about it and being too closely involved with the terrible affair.

They wanted to forget it. For the time being, at least. They wanted distraction. Most of all, they longed to be made to laugh again. There had been too many tears and sleepless nights.

Editors and publishers aren't fools. They don't reject manuscripts for the hell of it.

So light romances with tender, hopeful endings, humour, thrillers, stories set in sunny, exotic places - preferably on islands - were published in a flood. Historical romances came into their own again. They were safely distant from the bloody-stained, painful present.

That makes sense, doesn't it? It can easily be understood at this distance in years. But at the time I assure you it rocked our little boats cruelly. We found we'd forgotten how to write sweet romances; we'd forgotten how to write about having fun, about hope and the possession of a blythe spirit. We post-war writers were a sorry company - and, God, were we hard up! It took more than a ration of a banana or a pair of silk stockings to put the sun back into our sky. It wasn't very easy to laugh but we tried. And eventually we won. After all, the rent had to be paid. And we were determined to write stories and books that would sell. Lessons had to be learnt, and we learned them.

Sometimes it's difficult to get life and our writing in perspective. We simply have to regard rejections objectively, and learn what they can teach us.

One of the things we young post-war writers very soon cottoned on to was that readers wanted wild life stories. The awful antics of humanity at war had sickened them. They wanted to identify with the creatures of earth, sea and sky. With dolphins, seals and sea-birds, and with rustic hamlets untouched by war.

Because family life had been so cruelly disrupted, novels and stories about happy, united families were in demand.

And now - ?

What do we consider the public demand is for right now? Think about it. Study the kind of books that are proving to be best sellers - 'sex and violence blockbusters' is the way they're currently referred to.

What is the mood and the background of the stories appearing in our magazines? What do YOU want to read about today? Because you and I are part of the complex jigsaw known as 'Everyman'.

Bear in mind that none of us writes simply to please ourselves, although naturally we must feel keenly involved with the people and events we're writing about. One can't write dispassionately.

It's one of the most fatal mistakes a writer can make to 'write cold.' To remain distant and uninvolved. If *you* don't feel genuinely involved, no one else will.

FEEL INVOLVED

Of course there are the evergreens that are always popular with some sections of the reading public, and can be given a topical appeal by introducing the immediate scene through telling dialogue or action.

Popular settings that don't date are still hospitals, hotels, airports, wherever a fine old mix of people are gathered together, and which promise plenty of action of one kind or another.

And of course there are family relationships, which offer endless possibilities and can always be made topical.

Or again there are the high and low jinks that can be set against fantasy backgrounds, at luxury holiday resorts, and on air or ocean liners.

HOW GOES IT, NEW WRITER?

How are you coming along so far?

If you feel dispirited now and then after trying your hand at writing a short story, remind yourself that you're in good company. If only you knew how often almost all writers have to face discouragement, pick themselves up, and carry on typing!

Writing is seldom easy, especially when you're new at it, but it does come more easily as you plod on. Believe me it does! And the compensations for working on regardless of failure or discouragement make it all worth while. The rewards are fantastic - and I'm not just talking about financial rewards - rather, the all-round joy of fulfilment.

Who among the Literary Greats didn't have to struggle? Worth-while rewards don't come easily, they must be worked for long and hard in the vast majority of cases.

Read their life stories when you're feeling discouraged. It will give you fresh courage, hope and inspiration to go on.

Nor is writing and finding markets any harder today than it ever was. Editors have never had more space to play with, or kinder hearts, than they have today. Their space is circumscribed, and they're tough cookies - because that's part of their game. They have to be to make a success of their exacting positions.

Don't waste your time wishing the writing game was easier. Or day-dreaming your life away. *WAKE UP AND WRITE!*

WHERE IDEAS COME FROM

Before we leave this important subject, let's look more closely at the fascinating challenge of recognising ideas when we come across them on our daily round.

When I say that ideas are everywhere, constantly, and that all you have to do is recognise their potential, pop them into the forcing box of your mind, and hatch them into plots that you can clothe in words and send forth in due course as stories, I mean just that.

Imagine - you wake up in the morning. You switch on your radio or television. And there, would you believe it!, are those persistent idiots working away at their morning exercises, or jogging round the block or the park before work.

Surely there is an idea here. In fact there are dozens of ideas right at hand if you can stop being irritated for a moment, and give a little thought to the consequences of a world-wide exercise craze that's got everyone on the go.

Imagine how a muscle-bound giant was intimidated by a fitness freak.

Or it could be a wife confined to a wheel-chair, while her husband fanatically pursues physical health. Just think of the interplay of emotions and relationships in this situation.

There could be a motherless child whom the father adores, whose future health, education or security depends on the man winning a fight or a physical challenge he fears. It could be a disease that threatens the man, of which only he and his doctor are aware.

Picture the strong man. Get right into his skin. Think of the things that could threaten his life, his mind, his security, his happiness or a precious relationship. They're endless, aren't they?

HEADLINE STORIES

Then turn to your morning paper. See how the headlines leap out to present you with ideas galore?

Or, if you haven't your paper handy, look at mine.

Staring straight at me from where it's been tossed on my desk is this headline:

'SHE'S MY DAUGHTER, MY LONG LOST FRIEND.'

It's about a man without a family. He lost them when his wife walked out on him - his gambling and general fecklessness drove her to it, I read, and the story is written by the husband himself, Jeffrey Bernard. The wife took their little daughter with her when she left him. Now the girl is 14 and ‘a poppet’, and father and daughter are building a friendship from scratch.

That interests you? You want to know more about these people? All right. So do I. It's an intriguing situation.

‘Now I'm starting to see her again after years. And she's suddenly like a long lost friend. It's like finding something treasured that you've lost and regained....’

So, there you are, a one-parent family without a family. She has an excellent mother who can combine love with discipline, a good step-father, and a father who tends to frequent betting shops and pubs more than he should.

‘All in all, I'd like to hug her to death. I hardly know her, and yet I love her as dads, I suppose, do.

'Most of all, I like to think that one's children can become friends. Like husbands and wives, children and parents work when you actually like each other. Love isn't enough, is it?'

Can't you recognise there the material for a darned good story - or even the germ of a novel? Think about it...

NEIGHBOURS AND STORIES

There's another headline story in this morning's paper that has shaken me badly. It concerns a neighbour of mine, although we have never exchanged a word, or even a nod, and I'm sure he has never even noticed me - noticing him - as I passed by his rather grand house two doors down the street.

I noticed the handsome young man because of his obsession. He owned a magnificent silver Rolls Royce, and he was constantly polishing it, flicking dust from its bonnet, making the windscreen and windows shine, or just standing back with his head tilted, loving the thing as it stood at the kerb outside his house.

It used to fret me that the beautiful monster spent his days and nights out in all weathers. There was no garage. What would the rain and snow and ice do to it? Let alone the exposure to thieves who are forever breaking into cars in our street.

But most of all I thought of its owner whenever I saw the car - and he was often right there to fill the picture, too. Wasn't he rather young to own such a car? What work did he do that he was so often fussing around during the day? Had he a family - I had never seen anyone else come out of the house -? You know the idle curiosity naturally nosey people feel about their neighbours? Nosey? Well, writers anyway.

Now all has been revealed, in the most tragic way. For one of the tyres of the silver Rolls Royce burst yesterday when the young man was driving into London - and he died instantly. I had a real sense of loss and sadness. The young man dead. His beloved car a wreck. I'm glad he didn't see it. I'm glad he took a vision of it in all its elegance, to heaven.

Because the story is here in this morning's paper, I now know a great deal about my neighbour. He owned a night club. He had a large family for rather grand cars have been driving up to his empty house all morning, and dark haired, youngish men have been slowly getting out of their cars and entering the house for a short time.

There's a story there sure enough. When the sadness has gone, and the pieces come together in my mind.

EVERY STEP OF THE DAY

The 'phone rings as you sit down to breakfast, one eye on the clock, as usual. Wrong number! But wait. Instead of feeling irritated, think of the possibilities there are in a wrong number being dialled at a precise moment.

It could be a matter of life - or death.

It could be a humorous or a shocking coincidence - someone from your past reintroduced by a dialling fluke.

It could spell romance. Or the death of a romance.

It could lead to all kinds of misunderstandings - well, just think about it. Your wife or husband is listening in to the conversation on the kitchen or bedroom extension... Or is it your mother-in-law, your son or daughter?

Endless possibilities...

And so the day goes on, step by step, as every day does. This is no different from any other day except that you're aware of the ideas that are falling ito your lap all the way. And I hope being jotted down in that notebook of yours for future development.

Let's pick up one of the many ideas you've gleaned from this morning's headlines, and follow it through.

Diamond-running. It's been blown up into a big story, and tied up with another on the same subject, although it happened in quite another part of the world. That means that the subject will be really hot. Not only blondes will be thinking about stones that are a girl's best friend. Diamonds will be in many peoples' minds when they put down the morning paper.

The subject is weighed down with possibilities of drama or tragedy - or humour. Perhaps tragi-comedy would be a good line to take, as it was in an excellent story I recently read by Daphne Ballard, called *'Night Stop'*.

A STORY ANALYSED

This is how *'Night Stop'* opens:

'They had been flying over the desert since dawn, and now the hands of the flight-deck clock were nearly half-past nine.

'The passengers were fagged and edgy after the strain of departure from England, and a sleepless night. They slumped this way and that in their seats, unrevived by the breakfast of sausage and eggs that had been served to them under the white-hot equatorial sky. The smell of it hung about still, a miasma clinging to curtains and upholstery.

'Ryan, co-pilot, came out of the flight-deck and walked the length of the plane in his shirt sleeves, surveying the double line of listless figures out of bloodshot eyes.

'The only ones with any spark left were the six-month-old baby, bolt upright and wide-eyed in his carry-cot, and Mrs de Fries, the incredible old ramrod of a woman in seat 25.'

You know that things are going to happen to these two people, the exhausted airman with the bloodshot eyes, and the alert old woman. And happen they do. Right to the clever surprise ending. A strange, tender friendship is built up between these two characters, which ends when Mrs de Fries is arrested at the airport. Or will it continue after the author has completed her short? This is how the story ends.'

'She took Ryan's hand in hers, and he felt her rings cutting into his fingers... He uncurled his fingers and glanced down. Winking up at him from his palm, where she had pressed it lingeringly into the flesh, was a blue-white diamond prismatic and dazzling in the night lights of Khartoum.'

The writer gave full measure of suspense and entertainment, as promised in her opening words. Not for a moment, until the very end, did the reader imagine old Mrs de Fries was a diamond-runner.

The simple idea behind that story was diamond-running. Give it a little thought, flush out a few memories of stories you've heard over the years, or stories you've read about diamond smuggling, and I don't doubt but that you'll come up with several plots for stories on this very subject.

A VILLAGE IN THE SKY

Every day there are ideas for all kinds of stories to be picked up from the papers. Some appear in the course of interviews, or originate in courts of law, from school reports, picket lines, farming communities, or social documentaries.

You can't take a step outside your door without coming face to face with a wealth of ideas, waiting to be picked, if you live in a highrise block of flats. These flats are like a village in the sky.

You can be quite sure that there's a human drama being acted out in every flat, for every floor has its group of families or of single men and women, from students to lonely old pensioners.

The countless ways in which their lives interplay is a forcing ground for good ideas which writers can work upon.

If you use your eyes and ears, you'll come across them in the lift, on the stairs, or you'll overhear them through thin walls.

Watch the kids being taken to school; teenagers going out to a disco or cinema in the evenings; see what you can read from the way parents go to work or to stand in dole queues, and how they return home at the end of the day. Watch with compassion, and try to understand what's going on in their hearts and lives.

They all have ideas for you to develop in your own way. But it's up to you to recognise them and work on them.

* * * * *

Of course you don't have to live in a busy city to have a quiverful of ideas. Farming or village life can be just as fruitful.

GATHER IDEAS

In an 'IDEAS' file or large notebook I want you to begin to seriously collect ideas for your stories. Write them down, or cut them out, and then file them. One day you may well find them priceless.

Take any one of the following headlines, sift it for ideas, and work one of these ideas into a plot. If possible, go on to write a story round it. These loaded headlines have all been taken from just one of today's papers...

1. 'I POISONED HIM DROP BY DROP'. Court hears wife's confession.
2. THE DREAM BOB BUILT. Bobb Blacker built a 3-storey block of flats single-handed - all 160,000 bricks of it. He plans it as a retirement investment.

3. DAUGHTER MISSING. So immigrants cancel flight.
4. SHE'S HAPPIEST UP IN THE CLOUDS. Pilot-Schoolmarm.
5. MATHS FORMULA WINS JACKPOT.
6. WOMAN JUDGE JAILS FARMER FOR SEVEN YEARS.
7. NOBODY EVER KICKED SAND IN HIS FACE.

Are you beginning to get the idea? Is plot-gathering becoming a fascinating challenge for you? Believe me, it could well change your life, as it has so many.

Writing can, in time, become a round-the-clock obsession. It can be fun. And it can pay off, bringing you fulfilment, success, financial independence. It's up to you!

* * * * *

CHAPTER FOUR

CHARACTERISATION

In this chapter we're going to find out how to make our characters live.

Think for a minute or two of the life-long friends who came to you in the first place from the pages of story-books.

How much richer our lives have been because these friends walked into our lives from the printed page, or were introduced to us at our mother's knee.

It seems incredible, when you think about it, that you've never actually met some of them in the flesh, doesn't it? They're so familiar. We know them so intimately.

Some of these literary friends have influenced our thought and broadened our understanding. They're great characters. Living people.

But remember they were born in the minds of the writers who conceived them. They weren't plucked from the pages of history, or dragged in from the street or the market place.

How did those writers achieve the miracle of infusing life into imaginary characters?

That's what we're going to find out here and now.

NO PUPPETS, PLEASE!

Anyone can write about puppets. Stock characters acting out stock situations according to formula. But who wants to read about them?

Are you a James Bond fan? If you are, you'll probably feel that this man comes to life on page and screen, pretty unpleasant and larger than life though some of us may consider him to be. Many people - strangely different people most of the time - feel they can identify with him. That he comes to life for them.

But do you know why he apparently comes to life for so many of his admirers? I'll tell you.

It's because James Bond lived so truly for his author that, in time, he took possession of Ian Fleming. He ran his creator's life, and he ruined it, as Fleming freely admitted in his autobiography.

Oh yes, he brought Ian Fleming a fortune. Made him a millionaire. But the price he exacted was no less than the author's peace of mind, his health, and eventually his life. That's how real he was.

I'm not suggesting for a moment that you'll be running any risk to your health and happiness when you create living characters. James Bond was a ruthless character, and Ian Fleming a particularly vulnerable man.

I just want to illustrate how very much alive a character can become to the writer who creates him. And that it was because Bond lived for Fleming, that we feel we know him in spite of his larger-than-life antics, and accept him as a credible person.

Are you wondering how the miracle is achieved? It's something every serious writer has to find out.

It's all in the mind, of course. The mind of the writer. That's where ninety-per-cent of a writer's work is done, with only ten per-cent at his desk.

Which means, you see, that we never stop working. Once we begin our writing career in earnest we find ourselves thinking as never before. In fact this part of our writing life goes on waking and sleeping.

We take our problems, our plots, our characters, our thoughts over into the hours of sleep, and our minds keep working away at them. Because, you will know, our minds never sleep. They keep working for us around the clock.

To infuse life into a character we have to think about him day and night until we know him intimately. Until, in fact, we can slip into his skin and experience his reactions to given situations. Until we can speak with his voice and dialect; walk with his gait; laugh, love, hate and dream as he does. Self-forgetting.

It really is quite a tall order, isn't it? But what fascinating possibilities are opening up for us.

Until your characters are fully alive for you, they must never be given free play in a story. Just be patient. Work on them. Think about them. And in time you'll find, I promise you, that they'll begin to live independent lives of their own.

Only then is it time to let them loose in your story.

Of course, you can write about them in the meantime. In fact I strongly advise you to write as much as you can about them even before you've breathed life into them. But not in a story.

As you think about your characters, visualising them, write pen sketches of the way they look, dress, walk, react. Write snippets of dialogue when you feel it comes from them, and not from you. It's so fatally easy to superimpose yourself, your mannerisms, prejudices, habits of action, on the characters you create. And this we must not do.

HAIL, CHARACTER, WELL MET!

Imagine meeting your character in a supermarket. What would he or she look like? What would they be wearing? And buying? Would they push through the crowd, or give way? How would they greet you - or would they give you the cold shoulder when you made some predictable remark about the way everything is soaring in price, or the tempting new line in cream buns?

Go on - live with them. Watch and listen to them. And, most certainly, practice writing about them.

Everyone expresses themselves in their own individual way. In dress. hair-style, favourite expressions of speech, little mannerisms, some of which would endear while others irritate. When these small pen-strokes are introduced naturally, they can help sharpen the image surprisingly.

Your characters will express themselves in all kinds of large and small ways - if you let them. In their home backgrounds, in the colours they choose to wear and to live with. Even in the perfume and shaving cream or after-shave they use, or don't use. You should know all these things, as their creator.

If your characters are going to live - and live they must - then conceive them in the round. In depth. Know all there is to know about them. Because, you may be sure, they'll be giving themselves away right through the story.

For instance, you're trying to bring a positive, joyous character to life. A young woman. All right. Do you know her? Can you see her dressing and undressing? Can you see her washing her hair or eating a meal? Can you see her room, inside her wardrobe and chest of drawers? Can you visualise her handwriting, and the kind of letters she writes - the sort of friends she writes to?

You must know all these things about her if she is to live - and many more.

Let me show you how Margery Sharp draws such a young woman. You're almost sure to be familiar with this writer's stories and novels - they provide good light reading that sometimes makes you smile while you're reading.

Well, here is her introduction to her key character in *'Something Light'*. Note how few words are used to build this girl up so that you feel that you know her, and certainly like her.

'Louisa Mary Datchett was very fond of men. Not all women are, not even those to whom matrimony is the only tolerable state; for these often like men as husbands, as other women like them as lovers, and others again as small boys. Louisa liked men.

'If a bus-driver halted for her at a pedestrian crossing, her upward glance was disinterestedly affectionate - there he was, hot and conscientious, minding his own masculine business, no awareness of her save as a possible hazard to his time-schedule - and there stood Louisa - liking him; and if on the island of her refuge she observed an old gentleman in a garish tie, striped red and yellow like a ripening pimento, her sympathetic imagination at once ranged over the whole field of English cricket, as she mentally wished him on to a happy day at Lord's.

'These examples, however, are merely illustrative. Most men were reciprocally aware of Louisa.' (Now read this carefully, please.) 'If she paid for her rangy height by cheeks thin as a whistling boy's, if her hair was turning like an autumn leaf - here a streak of cinnamon, there a dash of pepper - she had nonetheless only to stand still in any public place, at a bus stop or outside a telephone booth and, as to Red Riding Hood, up came a wolf.

'Yet did she respond, and Louisa usually responded, how many a wolf turned nursling! To be listened to (wife not understanding wolf), to be found employment (wolf out of work), to have musical instrument (wolf potential member of a dance-band), got out of hock! It was extraordinary how swiftly they appreciated her special temperament.

'Bachelors in lodgings going down with influenza employed their last spark of consciousness to telephone Louisa. Sometimes their landladies telephoned Louisa. She was constantly being sent for, like a fire-engine, or despatched, like a lifeboat, to the scene of some masculine disaster; and fond of men as she was, by the time she was thirty she felt extremely jaded.'

There you have Louisa. You know her, don't you? You can see her swinging down the street on some high-hearted errand of mercy.

You know how she walks, quickly and lightly, with a long free stride. You know how her hair and teeth and eyes shine. You know the kind of voice she has, warm and rather deep, with a laugh quite free from affectation or inhibition. Yes, you know this honest, attractive young woman.

And why do you know her? Because Margery Sharp knew everything about her when she pushed her out into the world to cheer us up.

TO START TO WRITE....

I'm going to say a little about a short story writer - in fact about two story writers, who are among the best loved in America.

The first is Robert Fontaine, and this is what he wrote for fellow writers to think about...

'To start to write is to start to live, because it is to start to observe and pity and love and adore and sing.'

He learned that from hard experience, this lonely young bank clerk who wrote because he had to write, in spite of every material and physical set-back, and with no encouragement for many years.

He wrote this, too:

'I was afraid of life and of people and yet I kept forcing myself to know them, to love and to hate them, to be with them and then to write about them. The more I thought about them and tried to understand them, the less I was afraid of them and the more warmth I felt for them.'

His very first ray of encouragement came from William Saroyan.

Fontaine was sitting, hat in hand, on the edge of a chair in an agent's anteroom, while around him the Press and the Agent and many loud and pushing individuals shouted and slapped backs.

'Who's that fellow out there?' Saroyan asked the agent. 'He looks like a nice guy, and an interesting guy. I'd like to meet him.'

The two young men shook hands and looked each other in the eye. And they were friends for all time.

Do you wonder Saroyan's characters live and breathe and tear your heart out? It's because his characters are a projection of himself. Characters always are. That's something we have to face, because often it hurts us to admit it. Nor carbon copies, obviosly, but no matter how objective we try to be, we project ourselves into everything we create - into everything we say and do; into our dreams and work.

PROJECTIONS OF OURSELVES

The characters born out of our minds, our hearts, and our infinite subconscious experience, whom we fashion and send out into the world for good or bad, are as truly part of ourselves as the flesh and blood children we bear.

And our responsibility for them - for the kind of people they are, the way they will influence other lives that touch them, is certainly no less because they've been born of our minds rather than our bodies.

This is something some writers have always understood. Charles Dickens knew, if anybody did, that one can only create characters by living them.

'I can't get on,' he cried once when he was stuck halfway through a piece of writing. 'I'm not of them. I'm still next door!'

You'll find that whenever one of your characters fails to come alive, it's because you haven't gone closely enough, or penetrated deeply enough. You've tried to manage a puppet show, instead of giving life - your life - to the character you're trying to create.

Manipulating strings may be very clever, but it's far removed from creative writing.

COMPOSITE CHARACTERS

Few characters are born solely in the mind of the writer. Usually they're a compound of people met, known, seen and imagined. That's why it's so important that we should jot down any odd facet of revealed character at the time we notice it. Before it's forgotten.

Paul Gallico spent many days before actually beginning a book, or even before writing a short story, working out details of characterisation on paper. He filled in every possible detail. And he certainly thought about his characters until they came alive for him.

This is vitally important because your characters must behave 'in character' under all circumstances if they are to be credible.

Recently I had the pleasure of listening to an interview with that splendid short story writer, V.S.Pritchett. At eighty-five he is as lucid, as humorous, and as productive as ever he was. It isn't surprising that he's considered one of the greatest short story writers of today, if indeed not THE greatest living story writer.

Yet he remains as modest and untouched by his considerable fame as when he was a young man striving for success.

He was asked how he kept young in mind and heart, and why the characters he brought to life in his stories today are so in step with the times.

'I've a lot to thank my grandchildren for,' he said, a smile in his voice. 'And I keep my eyes and ears alert constantly. Nobody in Camden Town, where I live, knows that I write. Why should they? To them I'm just 'old Mr Pritchard,' part of the local scene. We're friends, and I can watch and listen and chat to everyone quite freely. It's a great privilege, which I enjoy!'

When he was asked the inevitable question, what advice he would give a young writer, he said:

'Don't invent, REMEMBER.'

And obviously, the more experience you have to draw on, the more there will be to remember.

Which brings us to the point of your personal identification with your characters.

I've said that this must be so close, so intimate, that you breathe the very breath of life into their nostrils. You create them of yourself - out of your mind, your heart, your imagination, and most of all from your experience and observation.

Very well. But don't make the mistake of superimposing yourself into the minds and actions of your characters. They must live independent lives of their own. This is most important. These are individuals you're sending out into the world. They must behave and react in *their* character - not yours. It is subtle, but vital that we understand this point.

Different writers tend to create different types of character, which is quite natural. Although often the same writer will be able to create quite different, and often very complex characters.

Well, look at the members of your own family - and your neighbours. Everyone is an individual.

Just think of the characters John Creasey usually creates. Positive, strongly drawn, not at all complicated.

You may be interested to know that John Creasey has had 385 books published to date, and another 50 paperbacks, and it's fair to say that the regular six to fifteen-thousand words he writes or dictates every day eventually appear in print. Daunting, isn't it?

This writer's greatest mental work has been in creating the characters that have become world-famous. He has often said so.

If you like his type of books, but have reservations because they're peopled by what are often referred to as 'stock characters', remember that they seem so mainly because you've seen them paraded before you in print and on the screen so often.

They are actually no more stock characters than any of your relatives or friends are 'stock'. They're merely familiar to you. Predictable.

Creasey wrote first to amuse himself as a boy when he was forced to lie on his back for many months recovering from polio. He found writing so fascinating during that lonely time that he has never stopped. He says it is as natural and as vital to him as breathing.

Between the ages of 10 and 17 he collected 743 rejection slips. Just think of it! But it didn't stop him writing. He didn't get his stories into print until he was 21, but those years of hard application at the writing game laid the foundation for his subsequent remarkable output and his fantastic success.

HE NEVER LOST HIS INITIAL ENTHUSIASM.

You mustn't think that because you didn't start to write until you were - well, whatever you were, it's immaterial - that you're handicapped and will at best limp in as an also-ran.

I don't know the actual statistics, but I'd be surprised if the majority of writers really got started on a career of writing before they were in their thirties. I don't mean doodling around with infrequent jottings in a diary, or endless high-flown letters to all and sundry which showed what a clever-dick you were with words. Many people find sublimation in this kind of pointless time-wasting.

Most successful writers I know through their work only began to write in earnest when they'd amassed a wealth of personal experience one way or another, and had read widely and thoughtfully, and when the urge, the desire, the compulsion to get some of it down on paper, took their lives over.

How can one hope to pour clear water from an empty vessel?

UNSUSPECTING WRITERS

If you want to create a character who will live with you and work for you through the years, perhaps for the rest of your life, go ahead and see what you can do.

But usually such characters prove that they've come to stay only after they've been launched, have caught the heart or the imagination or humour of the reading public, and the cry goes up, 'Give us more of this man or woman or child' - (or it could even be an animal).

It has to do with the magic of Timing, which we considered in ost chapter, remember? The Time and Mood were right.

Characters who first featured in short stories, and then in collections of stories, in television series, and then perhaps in films, are the best examples.

Quite a few of them have been charismatic private detective types, like Father Brown, Sherlock Holmes, Miss Marples, Adrian Mole. They were all born to unsuspecting writers, and took over the control and direction of those writers' lives from then on to a great extent, usually with very happy consequences to all concerned.

Do you notice how all these 'stickers' have spirit? How they exert their positive characters? You'll find no colourless, wishy-washy, predictable 'stock' characters among them.

OUR RAW MATERIAL

Wherever you were born, wherever you now live, be sure of one thing, you're peculiarly fortunate in the raw material you have right at hand to work with - as a writer.

Never bemoan the fact that you're not living in the exotic Far East, or on a South Seas island. Wherever you are you can bet your life it's rich in natural literary gemstones which just have to be located, mined, and polished.

Take my homeland, South Africa. I once heard an enthusiastic young writer from another country exclaim, 'Boy, is this place loaded! There's so much wonderful material for stories here, I don't know where to get started!'

How right he was. And he later proved it by writing some excellent stories and books based on various aspects of life in Southern Africa.

And yet how many indigenous writers cry defeat because they believe publishers and editors rule out South African subjects and characters - and writers.

What a good thing Wilbur Smith, Athol Fugard, Laurens van der Post, Andre Brink and Uys Kringe didn't let such negative thoughts inhibit them. Like Nadine Gordimer, they appreciated that writers have been given a unique opportunity to use Time and Place, where violent, strange history is in the making. And that they have an important part to play in writing, truthfully, about what they know at first handle in Africa or an English village, in Tibet or the heart of Paris, be sure of one thing - the raw material is all about us from which good stories and books can be built and carefully, passionately, crafted.

I suggest that you stake a claim, wherever you may live in this wide, wonderful world. And go right ahead and mine it for characters, for plots and action, giving it everything you have in you to give. Right here is where the grass is greenest - make the most of it!

SLANTED REVELATIONS

Your characters should reveal themselves by their speech and actions. They shouldn't be described, explained, or pointed at by you, the writer.

This process of self-revelation should, in fact, be taking place quite naturally in all kinds of ways throughout your story.

For instance, instead of describing your key character like this:

'She was a frail woman, shrunken with age,' wouldn't it be better to let her image come across naturally through the action, something like this:

'She looked up into the face of the man she hadn't seen for fifty years, and steadied herself against the chair he had carved for their first home.'

There the reader has been told, naturally and clearly, not only that she is in fact old and frail, but their tragic relationship is hinted at. The reader's curiosity is captured. What could have parted this man and woman all those years ago? What will happen to them now?

You want to describe your blue-eyed heroine, still a charmer in spite of five years of marriage on a shoestring, and a couple of children.

Forget all about the colour of her eyes and growing lyrical about her vital statistics.

Instead, why not sit the young woman in front of her mirror and let her 'give herself away.' Perhaps something like this:

'She smoothed the dress down over her hips and studied the effect in the mirror. Not bad! Thank heaven the diet had worked like a charm. She had only to take up the hem to make the dress wearable.

'If only the kids hadn't broken the bathroom scales she would have had the satisfaction of confirming that lost weight. At least it was enough to make it possible for her to wriggle into the old frock for tonight's celebration.

'It had been Tom's favourite. But what man doesn't prefer blue to any other colour? She remembered that he had remarked that it had exactly matched her eyes. Would he remember that? There had been so few opportunities to dress up and celebrate in the past five years. But perhaps, after tonight - '

Your readers will know that a character is tall if someone has to look up to him. Or if he instinctively ducks his head on entering a cottage doorway.

They will know that he's a shrimp if someone spots his bald patch when they're both on their feet.

I'm sure you get the general idea.

DON'T WASTE A PERSON

Every person you see, you meet, you live with, or you read about - learn all you can about them and from them. Don't let your personal prejudices and feelings come between your understanding of human nature. Try to understand others as thoroughly as you can. We're not carbon copies. Every one of us is unique.

How can we possibly create people unless we know them? Remember, every new person you meet can be an encyclopedia of emotions, just waiting to be read by you, and then stored in your growing bank of experience out of which your characters, your very own people, will emerge.

You should do this work when you're waiting for a bus or for someone to serve you, when you're spending time with relatives, friends or others, while all the time you're aching to get back to your writing.

Just remind yourself that writing doesn't begin and end at your typewriter. It goes on all the time. Anywhere.

Watch the way people walk, use their hands, carry parcels or babies or flowers - and put it into words in your mind and notebook. Watch the way people look at each other, the way they dress, eat, and laugh or cry - how would you describe it to your readers so that they feel they're watching it too?

Listen to the way people talk, and breathe, and sing and eat - you'll be writing about it one day, so take careful note now.

Conscious research is done in the mind, unconscious research in the heart. Both kinds of research are vitally important to the writer.

William Blake wrote: 'A fool sees not the same tree that a wise man sees.' And you could also say that 'a writer sees not the same tree, the same sunset, or playing children, nor does he experience the same joy, the same sorrow, that a non-writer sees and experiences.'

It is this ability to see things in a special, intimate, lasting way which is, in essence, unconscious research.

BACKGROUND AFFECTS CHARACTER

The short story writer, Percy Lubbock, naturally appreciates the importance of creating characters that live. He has a most interesting technique. It could help you.

He thinks about a story until he can see it as a play, with the characters revealing themselves as living people on the stage of his mind. He watches them 'perform', noting every detail.

He says, 'We speak of telling a story, but the art of fiction doesn't begin until the writer thinks of his story as a matter to be shown, to be so exhibited that it will tell itself.'

And he goes on to explain in his book,*'The Craft of Fiction'*, that by seeing a story as if it were a play, not only does it come alive, but it also makes it impossible for the writer to 'go into those long, dull dissertations about people and props and places, that simply put the kiss of death on a manuscript.'

So the curtain goes up on your scene - a scene so familiar to you through much thought that you'd recognise it anywhere, at any time. And your characters at once get into their stride, simply because you can see them so clearly, and you know exactly what they have to do before the curtain comes down at the end. You're on stage with them - you are one of them, involved in the action.

Characters draw life and actuality from their background. If it's merely a painted backcloth then they'll appear contrived and lifeless, too.

The writer must feel involved and familiar with the scene in which he sets them. In imagination he must have walked in the same parks and street, haunted the same shops and beaches, climbed the same stairs to bed; he must know the colour of the living walls and the names of his neighbours, as well as their habits and characteristics. Even though such detail doesn't come into the story, HE MUST KNOW IT PERFECTLY.

In short, he must be as intimately acquainted with all the details of the scene as the characters would be in real life - even thogh he never has to actually mention them in his work.

He must really know how and where his characters live at home and at work. Only so will he be sure that the world he creates is built on solid foundations, and can he be sure that it will carry conviction to his readers.

* * * * *

Our next chapter will be devoted to descriptive writing, and then we'll go on to study much more deeply the subject of the interplay of background and character. It really is a subject with wide, deep implications, and one we must thoroughly understand.

Meanwhile I suggest that you do your research along these lines. Make notes of the things you learn. The many ways in which each one of us impresses our personality on our surroundings, for instance. The way we expose ourselves through the care, neglect, decoration or arrangement of our material background.

Think of the many ways in which our background influences our approach to life and our fellow man.

For instance, you wouldn't expect a slut to come from a well-ordered home, would you? Quite regardless of whether it was one room in a poor street or a gracious home in a select neighbourhood.

Nor would you be very likely to find a well-adjusted, industrious, tranquil person come from a broken, tragic home, and general disorder.

You'll find that one is frequently surprised by the seeming incongruity of personality and background, but by probing deeper an explanation will usually become apparent.

When you study these fellow travellers, or the men and women you work with, try to build up a mental picture of the homes they come from - the jobs they're going to or coming from.If possible, without giving offence by what might be construed as inquisitiveness, check and find out how wide of the mark you were - or how near.

Listen to people. Let them open their hearts to you if they will. Have time for others. Apart from the fact that you should do anyway if you're a genuinely caring person, you may well acquire a reputation for being wise, courteous, charming - if you're lucky! - but you should certainly learn truths that will be invaluable to you as a writer.

If this seems a rather cynical attitude, I don't mean it to be. Our interest in others should always be sincere and compassionate.

People need to unburden, and who better than to a stranger? A stranger who will listen to them and respond with kindness. And then pass out of their lives.

You do get the idea, don't you?

Watch. Listen. Record. REMEMBER!

And there's another important point to bear in mind. When you're reading the paper, remember that you're reading stories about other people. People like yourself, with human frailties, ambitions, loves and hates. Try to put yourself in their place. Think - 'This could be happening to me!' - whatever it was that had shot these people into the headlines.

Imagine how you would have acted in similar circumstances - try to be truthful with yourself. How would you have felt? What would you have done?

Try to understand. And never stand in judgement.

PUT YOUR CHARACTER ON ICE

I can't overstress the importance of writing character sketches from life. We all have wonderful opportunities to study those about us at home and work and play, as well as family, friends, neighbours and mere acquaintances. Make the most of it.

If you haven't already started a file of these closely observed CHARACTERS, open one now. It will be a goldmine to you in years to come. In fact I don't know a serious writer who hasn't captured and filed a host of characters for future use.

I've just brought out one of my bulging 'CHARACTERS' files and chosen one at random. I won't re-write or polish it up. Here it is exactly as I got it down.

It was typed many years ago, but as I scanned the pages the friend lived again as clearly as she came across to me then, and I find that I'm smiling and feeling light of heart - which was how I used to feel when in her company all those years ago when we were young, and life was pretty wonderful - especially when in her company.

It goes back to the war years, when my sister and I lived in Hampstead, North London. Two young, very green South African girls, living in the blackout, and shacking down in a tiny attic flat that was called a studio, because it happened to be in Hampstead.

I've called this girl Dolly Gray, although of course that wasn't her name. She's still very much alive, and pretty famous now, and for all I know she may be cloaked in respectability. We've lost touch ,but I often come across her in literary magazines. But this is how she was all those fleeting years ago:

'Our friendship with Dolly Gray has brought us unalloyed pleasure. I never meet Dolly without feeling happier for the encounter, and Sally feels the same. I imagine most people do.

Whenever one of us remarks, ‘I met Dolly in the High Street’, the other invariably chuckles or grins in shared enjoyment. We regard her as one of the joys of life - she never turns bitter or sour in the mind. She's simplicity itself in these complicated times. And she's nice.

Dolly is a hard indiarubber young woman, and she bounces from bed to bed with the greatest enthusiasm and good humour, and an air of innocent enjoyment that immensely becomes her. It never occurs to her to be discreet. She trusts the world with her open heart, and I can't see the world letting her down.

She enjoys the lusty variety of her love-life wholeheartedly, and to see her skipping down the steep High Stret hand in hand with her latest love, firm round rubber breasts bounce-bouncing, her skirts glued to her strong rubber thighs, is a sight to lighten the heart.

Her hair is straight and yellow, and burns with vitality. Her eyes are round and china blue, and as kind and guileless as a happy, relaxed, trusting child's. I've never heard her make an ungenerous remark, or known her do harm to a living soul.

She chooses her words with meticulous care and speaks them beautifully, enjoying the shape and sound of them, and using her mellow voice as she would a musical instrument. Her capacity for silence, for sympathetic listening, is unique.

There's no end to the list of her accomplishments. She's always proving herself in yet another field - as author, artist, social historian and lecturer, she's equally brilliant.

She can play the mouth-organ, sitting bare-footed and cross-legged on her studio floor; or bounce and fling herself through a host of folk dances. She can concoct astonishing meals as though by magic, especially in view of the tight rationing.

And she can make men happy. There's no doubt about that. Not for long, perhaps, although in this, too, she has it in her to surprise one. But always, whoever the fortunate man may be, while it lasts the relationship is a supremely happy one for all concerned - which means, obviously, the two of them.

As soon as the bright happiness begins to fade, with a great bound she's off, straight into another man's waiting bed. Her reserves of emotional and physical energy have so far withstood every test of the war, and show no signs of wavering.

And always there's another good man waiting to be loved and mothered and petted and charmed in turn by dear Dolly, and introduced without reserve or inhibition to the wide company of her affectionate friends.

She is, to my mind, the perfect challenge to coy advertisers of cosmetics, body garments and fashionable clothes. For she scorns them all, and yet she has more sex appeal than any other woman I know.

She trims her shoulder-length hair herself, snipping away absentmindedly with a pair of sharp, curved nail scissors - with which she also trims the bacon and her nails - and, while she talks or listens, she studies the effect of her snipping in whatever shiny object may be handy - a window, samovar, or the glass doors of a bookcase. I believe the only mirror she possesses is a convex 'magic mirror' that hangs on the landing, which has sustained a great crack across its face on one of the countless occasions when an exploding bomb has shaken the old house and hurled the mirror from the wall.

Caring nothing for conventions and, I suspect, having been conveniently born without any of the seven veils of inhibition, life, for Dolly, is essentially simple and carefree even in these frenetic times.

Her family are professional people and moderately wealthy. They deplore their daughter's promiscuous way of living, yet they love her despite it. Being typically English, they can gloss the whole thing over and pretend it doesn't exist.

They appear to find some consolation in the thought that once, when very young, Dolly legally married a respectable young man whose surname she liked well enough to make it her own for better and worse. So her family was spared a good deal.

She's ageless. My belief - and hope - is that she will somehow remain so. Even at the end of a night's fire-fighting she'd pass for twenty in the wan, unkind light of dawn. I know that her identity card reveals that she was born in 1902. It's quite unbelievable. But it makes no difference, anyway. The years have simply passed her by. Which gives one pause for thought.

Somehow, in the generous abandon of her living, she's found the mainspring of perpetual youth. Or so it seems. Dear Dolly!'

Although I haven't yet used that pen-sketch of my friend, how glad I am that I jotted it down at the time. Some day, perhaps, Dolly will walk into a story of mine and make it shine. Meanwhile - I recall so much, so well, thanks to those rough notes. Dolly still lives for me even though we haven't met for many years.

* * * * *

YOUR BOTTOM DRAWER

Is writing coming to you any easier now? It will, I promise you, if you persevere. It can't fail to.

And, no matter if you do feel that some of the stories you're turning out should be scrapped - don't do it!

Add them to those manuscripts you're storing away in your bottom drawer. There's every chance that when you go back to them and read them through slowly, pen in hand, you'll spot just where their weakness lies and be able to straighten and polish them into marketable stories.

I'll tell you this. Of the many professional, successful writers I know, there isn't one to my knowledge who hasn't occasionally turned out a flop. A story that's had to be put on ice for future revision and much more thought. And quite often these stories, that got off to such a poor start, have raced home as winners. I'm constantly hearing of such experiences.

By the way, you are reading a steady stream of short stories, aren't you? Analysing them as you go along? Learning from them? Because you must, you know. It's all part of the drill of being a writer. Thinking. Reading. Writing. Revising.

Here's a book I do recommend that you get - and study. It should help you tremendously.

The book is called *'Becoming a Writer'*, and it's by an inspired teacher of creative writing who is a household name in America, Dorothea Brande.

She has given the writing world a number of excellent books, and this new soft-back reprint is one of her best. As John Braine, who wrote the introduction to this latest edition declares: 'No writing can do without it.' It's a classic of its kind. Do get it.

I just hope a little of the promise and excitement - a little of the challenge - of this writing game is getting through to you by now, because, believe me, it is the most wonderful work in the world - if one is lucky enough to be a writer at heart.

It will never let you down. You can write in sickness and in health, wherever you are - even if rejection slips come thick and fast, and you remain as broke as you've ever been - your life will be enriched and broadened by the demands and experiences you'll encounter - as a writer.

But there is one thing I must say to you. UNLESS writing excites you for its own sake; UNLESS you're thrilled by the challenge and the hard graft can be accepted without question - find some other work to throw yourself into. The hope of winning fame and fortune simply aren't enough. You've got to be driven by a genuine inner compulsion, excitement, LOVE of writing, to be a real winner. Writing *demands* - only your best.

* * * * *

I'm sure you're going to enjoy our next chapter. The subject really is fascinating! DESCRIPTIVE WRITING, and TEMPO IN WRITING.

I suggest that when you strike a snag in your writing, you make a note of it rather than gloss it over. To do the easy thing would simply be to invite it to raise its head again on later occasions.

Having made a note of your problem will ensure that it won't be overlooked, and in this way a solution will eventually be found. And when it is found, mark it, and note it in your file where the original problem was written down. Another problem solved! Another doubt clarified.

And now - good writing! Success will certainly be yours - if you work for it. Not otherwise.

Risking repetition, let me say once again that you really must write something every day. And I do mean - every day! There really is *no* other way to build yourself up as a writer.

CHAPTER FIVE

TEMPO, AND DESCRIPTIVE WRITING

Here is something I've learnt from experience that may help you to put a little more zing into your stories.

Tighten up the pressure of your tempo.

We're so used to regarding Time as our enemy in our work, that it will be a new experience for you to look to Time for help.

If the hero or heroine in your story needs a large sum of money - and who of us doesn't? - and you've made this the core and the goal of your action, then tighten up the whole thing by making it imperative that the money shall be found TOMORROW. A life or a home or a career could depend on it.

You see how the tension increases at once? There is immediately more suspense and excitement, and the reader knows the action will be swift and will carry him along to meet the challenge.

There's so much uncertainty, so much hanging about in life, that readers enjoy quick, positive action in their stories. It's an antidote to everyday frustration. Pep it up!

Consider the challenge there is in sentences like these:

'You've two days to solve the murder!'

'Have the ransom money here by midnight or your child will die!'

'If I can't get my weight down by Saturday I'll never squeeze into my hired suit, and the wedding's off!'

'Unless he reaches the signal box in two minutes flat the Express will plunge over the broken bridge!'

TIME LIMIT

The Time Limit can be dramatic, humorous, magic, blood-chilling. Apply the pressure and see how action, characters and dialogue all stiffen up in response to the challenge.

This is something that's been known through the ages, of course, only, like all old tricks, when one finds it out for oneself it feels like original magic.

Think of the Children of Israel and how they had to beat the Time Limit through the Red Sea before the waters rushed together again..

And Cinderella, you remember, only had until midnight to land her prince, not a moment more.

You'll be amused to find how many character in literature have been geared up to beat the clock, and have won your whole attention because of this. You'll remember how effectively this ruse was used in '*Around the World in Eighty Days.*'

You won't be able to ramble on, using long-winded sentences, and padding your story with cotton-wool phrases and dialogue, with one eye on the clock.

You'll find that you experience the feeling of urgency yourself as you write, waiting for that clock to strike calamity or victory at a certain hour. The possibilities are endless.

Think of a fraught situation that has developed on an oil rig, and go to work on it.

There are countless situations offering drama for all tastes. You only have to read or tune in to news any day of the week to have a hatful of glittering ideas spill out of the news slot machine.

MAN VERSUS NATURE

Writers have been using the Time Factor as the magic wand in every kind of story, right back to the beginning of story-telling.

Can you wonder? Just think of the remarkable tension Nature imposes which men and animals have to try to outwit, and the object lesson it's been for writers ever since men told their tales on cave walls, leather and stone. This is the whole foundation of conflict which is so essential to every kind of story.

Just think now... There's the Big Freeze or the blizzard threatening the hunter, his pregnant wife, or a herd of reindeer.

Or a volcano's about to blow its top.

There's the forest, veld or prairie fire sweeping across the land before a high wind. Think of the wild life as well as the humans who could be trapped by the flames. It could even be a botanist vainly trying to save a clump of rare orchids from extinction.

There are the migrating birds, fishes and animals, intent on answering Nature's Call which has directed their lives through countless years - held up by hurricanes, drought, earthquakes, floods, or atomic explosions. Or blotted out by man-made polution of air and water.

Or you could have a time-bomb ticking away. Although personally I feel that that situation has been done to death in recent years, when a time bomb was discovered high up in the Eiffel Tower only yesterday, and defused in the nick of time, high drama was there right enough. It was all too surely of the present, and as horrific as it ever was or could be in the future in its implications.

Of course you could be as clever in your handling of the situation as Ken Bennett was when he handled the theme in his story, '*Time to Kill.*'

This is a gem of a suspense story, the characterisation of the two men involved brilliantly drawn, and the tension grips you almost unbearably as the story is told.

Just listen to the opening sentence. It's typical of the writing throughout the story:

'The gardens and courtyards of the Palais-Royal were as familiar to Aristide Leblancs as his bed or the faces of his children.'

Immediately, you're introduced to the setting and the key character. And every word is most carefully chosen, with utmost economy and the simplicity which high drama demands.

* * * * *

The Time Factor can work out in strange ways. For instance, when George Axelrod read that Robert Sherwood had stated that anyone who wanted to write a play should do so before he was thirty - what happened?

Axelrod looked at the calendar on his desk, and realised that he had just six weeks to go before his thirtieth birthday.

So he sat right down at his typewriter and hammered out 'The Seven Year Itch'! If he hadn't had that challenge, if he hadn't been impressed by the challenge of that Time Factor, he declares that it's most doubtful if he would ever have got around to writing the play that had been tossing around in his mind for years - or any other play, come to that.

He needed a jolt to get him going, and it got through to him and set him off through the Time Factor and the challenge it presented.

But of course the classic example of making the Time Factor work for you was shown in '*Around the World in Eighty Days*' What a challenge that presented to Jules Verne, and how dramatically he met it!

You remember how Phineas Fogg believed, near the end of his heroic journey, that his time had run out - and then, while the world of readers held their breath, the International-Dateline-Time-Factor gimmic saved the situation!

So use the Time Factor to quicken the pace and hold the interest of readers. It may well provide just that extra sense of suspense and tension that your stories need.

SCENES THAT LIVE

We must try to find out what it is that makes some backgrounds so real to the reader that they're remembered as actual experiences, while others convey no conviction whatever. And then let's go on to see how best we can capture Mood with the written word.

You must, at some time in your life, have experienced A Moment of Truth.

Some searing, desperate or sublime experience that has torn away the veils we usually drape around our consciousness - and we see what is really there. We see it clearly and in depth, without flinching away. And that moment remains with us forever, even though we sometimes prefer to cover it up again and ignore it.

You can be quite sure that it isn't forgotten. Go back to such a moment. Be brave - dig it out and look at it squarely. It may well take courage, for there are even some blissful Moments of Truth that take courage to face.

You recall the peculiar clarity of small things that you experienced then? How your sight, hearing, how all your senses were tuned up far beyond what is normal? So that you saw a leaf, perhaps, or a thread of cotton, or heard a bird sing, or caught the fragrance of a flower - and how different it was to the way it is normally. Which is blurred, half-seen, half-heard, only slightly felt.

It had the feeling of a revelation, didn't it?

I remember one such experience when I was caught in an isolated and unfamiliar London Square in a violent air-raid. It burst on us without any warning siren because of low-sagging cloud.

I dropped to the pavement and pressed myself against the cold red brick wall while the bombs screamed down and the earth rocked with the explosions.

And suddenly, between the deafening scream and thunder of one stick of bombs and the next, I twisted my head and saw a grey dove sitting on the branch of a small, perfect tree, every remaining leaf pure autumn gold.

The dove stood up at that moment, ruffled its feathers, made a gentle mother-sound in its throat, and then sat down again on its branch. That was all.

It was all gone when the curtain of dust rose after the next explosion - the bird, the tree, and the houses across the Square. All gone.

But I'd experienced every detail of it so that I shall always know the thud of that dove's heart and the warmth of its body... It will always be part of me. Not the bombing. That means nothing now. But the dove and the little golden tree...

Our heightened perçeption in times of great emotional test captures tiny significant details - for that flash we know the truth - and it becomes part of us forever.

Looking back, there are many such moments that come to mind, unaffected by the passing years.

I remember with living clarity lying face down on the burning ground of my childhood orchard, wracked by grief. Seeing with wide open eyes my tears fall on to the sun-baked earth. And a tiny brown ant pausing on its erratic journey to drink a salt tear before it vanished into the thirsty ground. In that moment we became fused as one, forever, that ant and I. And it brings the whole scene sharply into focus, the grief and the hopelessness and the hot sun on my body and the scent of white irises flowering nearby.

It is by pin-pointing small, vital details that you bring a scene to life in your mind and in your writing. Not by shovelling adjectives in with a heavy spade. Adjectives must be used to colour in your scenes *very* sparingly. Only then can they have any real impact.

Use the simplest words at all times in the simplest way possible. The very essence of good writing is simplicity. It's a sign of strength in a writer.

IDENTIFICATION

Your readers must feel identified with your characters, and no less with your settings.

They must feel they're experiencing the same actions that motivate your characters. You must present the scene so vividly that it will remain in the reader's mind as something he has actually seen. Just as your reader should feel he'd recognise your characters if they met on the street.

And the only way you'll contrive this kind of magic is by living the scene yourself.

You must think about a scene until you're in it. Until you can see, smell, hear every detail of that scene. And then you must stand back, as it were, and take the whole scene in, recording it on your inner eye in every detail.

I've found that it sometimes helps if I think of myself as a camera, focussing carefully on the scene I've built up with such loving care that it comes to life.

And, when you do that, what is it that catches your attention - because you must know how there is always a point of sharpest focus that catches your eye and rivets your mind, and anchors itself in your memory?

Is it the way the sunlight streams in through the window, bringing brilliant colour into the rooom, and giving the garden beyond a faded look by contrast?

Or perhaps it's the tiny echo of dazzle in the diamond earings of your heroine that links up with the blaze of the chandelier in the grand room?

Or the way a woman unconsciously twists a wedding ring on her ringless left hand?

It's by such small, carefully observed brush-strokes that you'll bring your scene to life. And you will only be able to do it if the scene and the characters live so clearly in your mind that these details spring out from the setting and claim your attention.

They can't be contrived. Not if they're going to carry conviction. Because only the truth can do that. And the truth must be felt by you, the writer.

INTERPLAY

Another thing which we have to thoroughly grasp and keep in mind is the interplay of character and environment.

Just as every word of our dialogue reveals something more of our characters or our plot, so the settings against which we make them take place, affect our story.

Think of a young girl in a summery field - perhaps waiting for her lover. There's a gentle blue sky overhead, the only sounds those made by bees, birds, and the lazy munching of a cow.

You wouldn't expect anything sinister to happen, would you? You'd know very well that the girl would be a 'nice' girl, that no booby-trap mine would explode under her innocent feet, no terrible tragedy would wreck her life at that moment. The mood is as bland as butter, and there isn't a quiver of tension anywhere. The reader settles down to enjoy a story of young love.

Now transfer that girl into a squalid slum street in a city. Rain is falling, the gutters choked with filth, and the girl is shivering in her threadbare coat.

The sounds include the blows of two men fighting in a dark alley nearby, the sharp blast of a police whistle, the approaching clump-clump of running footsteps, and the savage bark of a police dog. And - the girl at least is aware of this sound even if you haven't heard it yet, although you should have done - there's the thudding of her frightened heart.

You see how the girl changes in your mind's eye? Although not one word of dialogue has been written, you know pretty well how each girl will talk; you should also be able to imagine a little of the way her mind works, and have formed your own shadowy idea of the home life that has conditioned her up to that point.

This association of ideas is a very interesting study. But it's one that we must be wary of accepting at face value without question. That's in common with everything else to do with out writing, of course. We must be fully AWARE as we write.

We must be alive to the possibilities that are latent in our choice of setting. I can't overstress its importance.

You see this very clearly demonstrated in films and in the theatre.

Just think of any of Hitchcock's films, and you'll see how much this little wizard depended on his setting to get across the mood, the suspense of his thrillers.

Think what he could do with fog, and sewers, and lonely wharfs in foreign ports. Fingers of fear start creeping up your spine at the first wail of a fog-horn, and you automatically suspect every hunched character who glances at you quickly from under the brim of his hat or cap.

Well, you've the even greater magic of WORDS to work with.

And just think of the possibilities for drama and suspense in a disused mine shaft or a cave; the desert or marches; a crocodile-infested river; a snow or mist-shrouded mountain fastness.

We don't have to rely on sewers or bleak, rotting wharves for our suspense-filled backgrounds. The range of our settings for the action of our characters to take place, is limitless.

STRENGTHS AND WEAKNESSES

Each of us, as writers as well as individuals, has our own peculiar strengths and weaknesses.

One writer may find special delight in writing dialogue. Another portrays character with inborn ease. And there are those who have a natural aptitude for portraying character action. In just the same way as there are portrait painters, and there are landscape and seascape painters.

Whatever your particular gift may be - don't take it lightly. Don't imagine that, because you're a 'natural' writer of one kind or another, you don't have to work hard at becoming an even better one. Perfection is always a long steep climb ahead.

Work on your strengths as well as your weaknesses. Be aware of them both.

That needed to be said because, in the first flush of success as a writer, there's often a tendency to rest on one's oars, too aware of earned laurels. And whenever this happens, and I see this complacency in myself or others, it's a warning signal that shouldn't be ignored.

We know only too well that we're either forging ahead in life, or we're slipping back. We never stand still. So it's important that we are alert for the signals that will affect our work.

THE CHANGING GAME

Now let's study how background and character overlap and influence each other. It's something we have to bear in mind as we tell our stories. One can affect the other, and often change it.

For instance, you take the character who was born and who grew up in a city, and who then makes his home in the country for one reason or another.

There you have the very real effect of background on character. You also have the no-less-real effect of character on background.

There will certainly be subtle and even dramatic changes in the atmosphere, and probably in the appearance, of the old farmhouse stuck in the emptiness of nowhere, when the farmer's son brings his city bride to live there.

Just imagine some of the possibilities.

The girl could have been an actress or a dancer; or the spoilt only child of rich parents; she could have been a young woman hiding a desperate secret - or a young business woman used to comfort and efficiency, being hounded by a clock, and taking all the amenities of city life for granted.

I want you to picture each of these girls in such a situation. Can you see her on that isolated farm? Can you imagine her reactions to the comparatively primitive way of life, and the demands that will be made on her to adjust and cope? As well as the demands she will probably make on her country-bred husband?

Neither the girl, nor her farmer husband, nor the old farmhouse will remain the same, will they? And think of the impact she'll have on her in-laws! The interplay of one on the other, for better or for worse, is bound to bring about changes both in character and in setting.

A game I used to play to pass the long days spent in slow trains crawling across the Karoo when I lived in the Cape Province and my family were in Natal - it often took three days and two nights to make the journey - was trying to sum up the characters of the people living in the uniform railway cottages that were so often the only buildings at the Halts where the train slept seemingly for hours taking water en route.

Those houses had been identical when they were built. The gardens were exactly the same size, fenced in the same way. They'd been subjected to the same sun, rain and wind. But the difference in them was often astonishing.

The characters had changed their settings so that one revealed the other. They overlapped. And what a surge of joy I always felt if members of the family came out to prop themselves in the doorway, or hang over the stoep railings, and stare at the train without expression or apparent emotion. I could then check how near or how far of the mark I'd been in picturing them.

And the relief I felt when I came across one of those railway cottages where the washing had NOT been draped over the rusty barbed-wire fence to be torn by the rough winds that blow across the wide flat land of the Karoo!

I always felt quite certain that the wife in that house must have come from a town where clothes-lines had become an accepted amenity.

We weren't into washing-machines and spin-driers in those days and areas, which was no hardship. I've always thought that one of the most comforting sights in the world is a lineful of washing flapping in bright sunshine. It warms my heart just to think of it, and the cosy smell of sun-dried clothes.

We know how that remarkable Quaker woman, Elizabeth Fry, changed a whole neighbourhood when she insisted on living in a tenement in one of the most demoralised slums in London. How her example was reluctantly and slowly followed when she washed her windows and scrubbed her steps. She showed the world the stuff Quakers are made of. They just never give up!

Elizabeth Fry went right on with her sweeping and scrubbing, and helped her beighbours when they would allow her to help, all done with great good humour.

Gradually her example caught on. And we know how, in the end, the changes which she brought about in that district were talked about in Parliament, and drew world attention from social reformers; how her influence spread to neighbouring streets and districts, as self-respect and pride grew, and Elizabeth Fry was able to close that chapter of her life's book, and tackle prison reform.

And, if you've read this amazing woman's life story, you'll know what she did to character and setting *there*!

DOWN TO EARTH

So you see how vital it is that we get to know the nature and the atmosphere of the scenes we present? As well as the background sounds and smells that accompany them.

It will all work together if you make your stories come alive - those characters of yours living and talking as naturally as they would do in life, and your backgrounds also living as winds breathe over them and storms shake them as the seasons come and go, and buildings and bridges go up or are torn down. Constant interplay, constant change, growth and decay. Bear it all in mind.

There's not a moment when something isn't happening around us. It's up to us to keep track of it and understand the why and the wherefore.

It's the ever-changing character of life that we must be aware of and present in words. And, as I've said before, we will only come to know it by getting right inside and looking out - by experiencing the 'feel' of the changes ourselves.

This is an exercise I do whenever opportunity presents itself. I've always done it and I expect I always shall, because there is so much to learn from the smallest thing. Like changing skies and the music of flowing water, the scent of flowers, and the wind in the trees and the grass. How much do we know about any of these things? How can we describe them so that they live?

This is what I suggest we writers do whenever we possibly can, no matter what the time and place.

We must be still, and watch and listen, rivetting our full concentration. And we must record what we see and hear, what we smell and feel, writing it all down or, if we are alone, using a tape recorder.

We must never stop being a listener and observer. In time it must come to us 'as naturally as the leaf to the tree.'

For instance, you sit alone on a sun-warmed rock on a beach, on a grassy bank in a field, on a park bench or in your garden. It may seem to you at first that you're all alone. But very soon the world about you will come alive for you. If you're patient and still, and really watching and listening with your heart as well as your ears.

You'll become aware of the warmth of that rock, the softness of that grassy bank, the tiny brittle sounds of the teaming insect world close about you; the glory of that pattern of sky, ever-changing overhead, with the flight of birds against it.

Nature will fill in your immediate world in the most wonderful way. Butterflies, ladybirds or minute creatures of the air, the sand or the earth will mistake you - so still! - for a natural phenomenon, and perhaps alight on your hand or crawl up your leg.

Learn to see everything at such times. To hear everything - insects, birds, grazing cattle, breaking waves that softly hiss as they fan out over the smooth sands; distant traffic. Feel the quality of the air as it blows or gently breathes about you. Smell every scent that wafts your way.

And then learn to make others see, hear, feel and smell what you are experiencing, through your writing. Some of my books have been translated into Braille, and when I keep this in mind it helps enormously to communicate my privileged experiences.

This interplay of Nature - of all of Nature, human, animal, vegetable, mineral - must be part of the language we learn and use. It must all be part of our awareness and understanding.

A STORY ANALYSED

I want to demonstrate what I've just been saying by breaking down a short-short story for you.

It isn't a new story by any means. It's been in my files for a long time, and I've read it with pleasure many times because it remains a rare little gem of its kind and can teach us so much.

It's called '*Monty Wakes In The City Of The Dead*', and it appeared in the magazine called '*TODAY*'. It runs to no more than 800 words, and describes an experience Monty lived through. There's no padding; no fancy words; just an acutely observed incident concerning fighting men, and showing how tension and actions interweave.

The writer was Gordon Thomas, world-famous writer and broadcaster, and every word is true. Another point; note his use of adjectives.

This short story has been selected by several editors of first rate anthologies as a little masterpiece of its kind..

'As dinner was served at a thousand tables the birds rose from their nests, wheeled over the sluggish city of Quetta, and headed for the surrounding plains. They flapped over the soldiers deployed on routine manoeuvres among the rocks. As the flocks passed, a nip came into the sultry air, and a soldier remarked that it was "real earthquake weather"'.

(There, in the first paragraph, you have the scene set. You have the period established. You have the first suggestion of tension and conflict in that reference to "earthquake weather".)

'A few miles away in Quetta's aloof Staff College - the backbone of the Indian Army - Betty Montgomery asked her husband to watch the skein of silk she was using for embroidery.'

(That tiny, significant point of focus.)

'He was the senior instructor at the college, a tireless, work-devoted man, who on that evening was six years away from immortality as Montgomery of Alamein. He looked at the silk. Their dinner-guest suggested that its appearance could be caused by electricity in the air. Every strand was separate and had become as stiff as wire.'

(Note the subtle introduction of the dinner-guest. No name was necessary so none was given, yet note the part he plays as we go on.)

'A quarter of a mile away in Quetta itself, few others noticed anything unusual on that Thursday night in May, 1935.'

(The easy introduction of the highly significant date.)

'The city of 20,000 was a caricature of the British way of life. 12,000 soldiers were stationed there, and their existence hinted at an esceptic Aldershot. But, like the RAF men at the modern airfield, they were there for a serious purpose. Quetta was the lynch-pin in British strategy in India and life within its confines was inbred, sporting and cheerful.

'By midnight, Mrs Montgomery had put aside her embroidery. Out on the plains the soldiers were glad of their greatcoats. The birds had ceased their cawing and were clustered on rocks away from the city, where the dogs still snapped and snarled at each other.

'The Montgomery's dinner-guest excused himself and went out to quiet his whining dog...

'5,000 miles away, in Farnborough, Kent, the guest's wife had a dream. She was standing on a rock overlooking a plain - as the Quetta Staff College overlooked a plain. Suddenly the sky grew grey. Cracks appeared in it, and she saw faces - black and white. A voice said "He's going to be all right!".

'In Quetta the man still struggled to pacify his pet, the soldiers shivered, and the silk remained stiff.'

(Note the close weaving of people, events, places? The steadily mounting tension?)

'Until 3 a.m.

'Thirty seconds later the city had its life torn out. The earth roared and shook over a cucumber-shaped area nearly 70 miles long and 16 miles wide. In those 30 seconds, 30,000 people were killed. But that man, as in his wife's dream, escaped.

'As he stood with his pet, not far from where the Montgomerys slept, he was aware that a great silence had come over the land. And then came a sound that reassured him - the short, sharp, army “alarm” call of duty buglers. He told himself that the situation was under control - and went to bed.

‘But in fact Quetta was a jagged, lifeless ruin. Its inhabitants either dead or buried under the rubble.

‘Out on the plains the soldiers stirred uneasily. They could see fires burning in the city. But their colonel dismissed the tremor as “unimportant”. It was only when a dispatch rider brought him an order to cancel maneouvres did he order his soldiers to go to the aid of the dead city.

‘Hours later, at breakfast at the Staff College, the tremors were treated as a joke. Nobody could see any signs of damage in the city.

‘The meal over, Montgomery drove at the head of a procession to begin another day's work. He talked earnestly to his companions about some military ploy and paid no attention to the surroundings until the car stopped.

‘He found himself in a Wellsian scene; all around him were wrecked buildings and rescuers pulling away the rubble... He could see damaged aircraft, crushed billets. And the line of blanket-covered bodies under some trees.

‘White-faced, Montgomery said, ‘We had no idea this had happened. What can we do to help?’”

(There couldn't be greater simplicity than that, could there? The one description, ‘white-faced’, conveys the shock the man had sustained. How many writers would have left it at that?)

‘What happened then is the greatest battle this military genius ever helped to plan and win.’

And then Gordon Thomas described the grim affair with the economy and control his tough writing life had taught him. He ended with this paragraph:

'This time of torment and terror was highlighted by the brilliance of men like Montgomery. Brilliance that not even bitter attacks by Indian politicians, who incredibly blamed the British for the earthquake, can tarnish. Maybe the politicians felt that Monty's wfe should have told them about the stiffening silk...END.'

* * * * *

You see how Thomas fastened on that tiny, vital detail of the reaction of Betty Montgomery's embroidery silk to the electrically-charged atmosphere, to draw the characters into the story, and rivet the mind? How, through this, he made the scene live, and awoke apprehension - tension - in the mind of the reader?

THE POETRY OF ONENESS

I want to finish this study of the interplay of characters and settings by quoting you something that will, I hope, explain what I'm trying to say.

It's taken from a South African story called '*The Miracle*', and it's about an old Bywoner (hired land workers sometimes referred to as 'poor whites') couple who are being turned off the farm where they've spent all their long, hard married life together, because the valley is going to be turned into a reservoir.

Their lives are being cruelly disrupted by their changing background - and you'll see something of the spiritual, mental and physical consequences brought about by this change of environment.

'Marta was sewing on the stoep when the sound of horses cantering over the iron hard veld reached her. Slowly she got to her feet, her sewing falling from her lap unnoticed.

'So it had come, this moment she had steeled herself to meet?

'The horsemen came in sight, Paul van Rooyen and a stranger, and Marta crossed the yard quickly to where Jan stood watching their approach.

"Do not be afraid!" she said, and slipped her hand into his.

'Paul van Rooyen walked his horse up to where the old couple stood waiting for him. He did not dismount, but leant down from the saddle to speak to them, seeing only an old man and an old woman standing together, hand in hand. More than that he did not see. The old man's shoulders that had once been broad were bent under the years of labour, but the head was still held high.

'Without a word the old couple heard what he had to say, and Jan took the paper which Meneer Paul handed down to him, but said no word. What may be said by a tree to the hand that uproots it? Marta reflected, remembering what Old Andries had said.

'Only when the sound of horses hooves had died away did either of them move or speak.

'It was the sudden trembling of Jan's hand in hers that roused Marta. She looked up into his face and a faint moan escaped her lips at all she saw and read there.

"Do not be afraid!" she said again. And the words came from the raging, tumbling river that was now her heart.

'As she hurried to the stoep to fetch a stool for Jan to rest on, she struggled for a foothold in the chaos that engulfed her.

‘She was passing beneath a peach tree, the stool in her arms, when she suddenly found firm ground under her feet. The turmoil subsided, and her heart was strong and again knew peace.

‘To Marta Marais the explanation was simplicity itself. God had spoken to her in His own way, and she had understood. The symbol He had used had been the single petal of a peach blossom which had fluttered down from the tree to rest on the woman's wrist.

‘The moment she saw the petal on the wrinkled, tanned skin she knew all would be well.

‘All her life God had spoken to her in this way, through the wind and the rain, the song of a bird, the momentary sharp focussing of a tiny veld flower, or the steady drone of a bee. She had never questioned; only understood.’

You see the interplay of Nature - of all of Nature, human, animal, vegetable, mineral - is, to my mind, part of the language of God. All part of the One Expression. It's when we accept the truth and poetry of Oneness, that our writing comes alive. Our settings must live as truly as do our characters. Because, in life, they do.

CHAPTER SIX

TITLES, DIALOGUE AND DIALECT.

You have probably found by now how each of us develops our own writing technique. Our personal approach to this business of writing short stories. Just as we do in everything else that we create in life.

I've known writers who always looked to the TITLE to set their creative wheels turning. They usually gathered all kinds of titles through the years, and paged through them whenever searching for the spark that could be coaxed to burn into the bright flame of a story.

Then again, some writers don't need to store collected titles. They have an inborn gift for choosing or shaping them whenever they're needed.

Of course, there are others who simply agonise over the choice of a title, and feel uneasy until one shapes itself in their mind as their story evolves.

They may well begin a story by climbing into the skin of a character, as many of us do, and living in it.

Or they may be natural architects, and begin by fastening onto an idea, and then built up their plot from very careful mental blue-prints.

LET TITLES WORK FOR YOU

Now the last thing I want to do is to convey the impression that one way of finding the right title for your story is right, and another way is wrong. We each have to approach this matter from our individual angle, and develop our natural way of working. It's usually a matter of trial and error. We must try each approach in turn, if we're uncertain, and then decide which is best for us.

One thing is certain. The title is a vital part of your story, and it must never be chosen lightly. If you admit to yourself that it really is little better than a label for your story, scrap it. It must be more than that.

Here are some qualities I suggest your title should have:

1. It should intrigue the editor and reader, making them want to go ahead and read the story.

2. It should be so fitting, so cleverly chosen, that it remains in the back of the reader's mind throughout his reading, adding to his enjoyment or understanding of the tale you've told.

3. It must harmonise with the tone of your story. That is really most important. You would never give a suspense title to a gentle love story, for instance, or a sweetly nostalgic title to a story concerned with blood and lust, or high adventure.

The Mood, the very nature of title and story must be in true harmony, and never convey a false impression of the unfolding story.

Unless you have a rare gift for choosing titles without the usual sweat and tears, I suggest that you collect titles in a notebook as some people collect jewels or rare coins.

Even if editors change your precious titles, as they frequently do - usually for reasons you may not be able to fathom - don't let that make you careless in your selection, shaping and polishing of subsequent titles. See if the change of title has anything useful to teach you.

There are many reasons why an editor may have changed your title - to do with the layout of the page, editorial policy, or the design, the overall appearance of the page. Or it could have been simply that what appeared to be a bright idea popped into the editor's mind, and he decided to use it. Never forget that editors, like publishers, are just ordinary mortals, although, like many writers, they seldom suspect it.

SOURCES FOR TITLES

Here are some of the obvious sources where you can look for good titles. I'm sure you'll find many others.

I remember Negley Farson explaining to us the sources he consciously tapped for inspiration in his writing. And he said that every one of his titles of his sixty-odd books and countless short stories had been taken from the Bible. It was a source he couldn't imagine ever failing him.

He had just come down through Africa, writing of his experiences on the way. And the title of the book that grew out of that experience came to him, as did all his titles, from the Bible. It was *'Behind God's Back'*. An excellent title for a book of travel and exploration.

If you're stuck for a title for a story you're working on, I suggest you see what you can find in the Bible.

To demonstrate my point I've opened my Bible at random. These titles danced to meet me, all of them on one page. They can be broken down, taking from them what one needs for one's purpose.

'FLY AS A BIRD TO YOUR MOUNTAIN.

LEST IT TEAR MY SOUL LIKE A LION.

IF THERE BE INIQUITY IN MY HANDS.

HE HATH BENT HIS BOW AND IT IS READY.

(THE BOW IS BENT).

IN THE NET WHICH THEY HID IS THEIR OWN FOOT TAKEN'

Each of those could be shaped into a fine title, or could supply the seed for a plot - nor, of course, is the Bible alone in providing ideas for good titles.

Turn to Shakespeare, or any of the great poets for ideas. You'll find yourself enchanted.

There are so many quotations containing either a simile or description of romantic love in such volumes that you need never be at a loss for unusual, lovely titles for your romantic stories and novels.

Nor are romantic titles all they can offer you. Think of some of the lines written by Edgar Alan Poe, for instance, or Dylan Thomas.

In an excellent book called *'Bartlett's Familiar Quotations'* there are actually three pages of small type in the index devoted to lines including the word 'love'. And any number of humorous, poetic or intriguing quotations that could be successfully adapted for stunning titles to fit any category of story.

"If Winter Comes' was taken from Shelley, and of course there are wonderful titles in Omar Khayam and any of the poets, past and present.

The Chinese novelist, Han Suyin, has a special genius for naming her novels. From *'And The Rain My Drink' 'A Many Splendoured Thing'*, and *'Til Morning Comes'*, to *'Winter Love'*, they are perfect.

Then there are the shock tactics a writer can use in his titles. Tom Kaye, the vital writer from Singapore, for instance, chose *'David, From Where He Was Lying'*, and *'It Had Been a Mild, Delicate Night.'*

While Robert Payne, that masterly writer of description, chose an almost hypnotic title for his hard punching novel about drug-smuggling in China, *'A Bear Coughs At The North Pole'*.

It was taken from a Chinese saying, 'When a bear coughs at the North Pole, they hear it in Peking.'

So TITLES is another file to add to your growing collection for future inspiration.

WORDS AND DIALOGUE

Now we're going to think about words. The most exciting and vital subject in the world for writers. Because words are the material with which we embody our creations.

Without words the people we create would remain locked in our minds. It is only by giving them the substance of words that we can release them from our imaginations and send them out into the world.

The importance of words can't be over-estimated. Nor the fact that WORDS LIVE.

It's a terrible thing when you find a gifted writer paralysed by the mistaken idea that words and grammar - the way words are used - are governed by set laws that can't be tampered with. That they must work with words as a stone mason works with chips of stone when he places them in careful mosaic designs.

Words aren't stones. Words are living things.

And because they live, they are constantly changing in weight, shape and shade of meaning. They are constantly being added to.

Of course there is no such thing as 'pure language'. How could there be? What do we mean by the word 'pure' anyway? My dictionary explains the word as 'Clean, uncontaminated, unmixed, unadulterated, chaste, upright, honourable, disinterested, unmitigated, simple, true, innocent, virtuous'. So what on earth do we mean when we speak - as some people do - of 'pure' language?

We assume they mean Unmixed, Unadulterated. Which, of course, is sheer nonsense. No language is unmixed or unadulterated.

Like the tides of air that blow across the face of the earth, so language blows and merges between man and man, between nation and nation, between one generation and the next. Constantly changing. Constantly growing to embrace mans' expanding consciousness and achievement. Their need to communicate.

I read the other day, 'Writing, as creative literature, is a vital link between the plan of God and the social progress of man.'

It is no more static, no more unchanging, than water or sky or the songs our hearts sing. Why, writing goes back to 30 or 40,000 years BC, when Paleolithic Man painfully told his stories with flint and vivid pigment in picture-words that described the dance, the chase, and the kill.

And, in the words we use today, we are still telling the story of the dance, the chase, and the kill. In simple words and with less toil and pain. But we're telling the same story, which is the remarkable story of man's experience here on this earth. And we're using words that have evolved, and which continue to evolve through the years. Ever changing.

The picture left by man down through the ages as he wrestled for articulation, is the spoor of history. A running commentary by our forefathers of life as it has unfolded through the years.

As writers, we must never lose sight of the fact that we're links in the endless chain of creative literature. There's pride and responsibility in the knowledge.

Every serious artist spends a great deal of time studying paints and pigments, and experimenting with them. But how much serious study does the average writer devote to mastering the beauty and complexity of his materials - WORDS?

We must experiment with the form and the grouping of words. Testing for clarity, for strength, for beauty. Trying to get out meaning, or our vision, across through the medium of words.

Only through thought, practice and revision can we achieve this to some extent.

DIALOGUE

No matter what stories and books you're going to write, you must study words and how to use them. Every craftsman must know and respect his tools. And words are the tools we use.

I ask you please to pay special attention to what I'm going to tell you now, because I believe it to be the very crux of Writing Dialogue.

You know the joy of reading prose that flows as smoothly and clearly as a valley stream. Sometimes in sunlight, sometimes in shadow, but always flowing smoothly from the page to the brain, with the image unblurred - crystal clear.

That's what we must aim to achieve in our writing - singing words.

Anything that impedes the smooth flow of the printed word to the comprehension of the reader must be avoided at all cost. Nothing must hold things up.

Will you keep that well in mind while we go into the problem that often troubles new writers. And some of us who are experienced, too. It's the problem of Dialect. The problem of when dialect should be used, if ever, and how it should be used.

Now I believe that dialect should be used *if it comes naturally*. You can't lay down any hard and fast rules here any more than you can in any other aspect of writing. We must present our characters faithfully and vividly. We must make them live.

And if it's natural for them to speak in dialect, then this must be conveyed. But it calls for great skill.

lt must never slow the pace of the reader, or raise questions in his mind. As you know, dialogue only looks and sounds true to the spontaneously spoken word. In actual fact it is not. And this is why:

DIALOGUE IS THE CONDENSED ESSENCE OF THE SPOKEN WORD.

You can imagine how impossible it would be for your characters to ramble on as we do in ordinary conversation. Your story would get nowhere. All the repetition, the stuttering and stumbling after expression, the extraneous chit-chat, the humming and hawing, has to be cut out, and your dialogue has to move your story and your characters along while yet seeming to flow quite naturally.

So, when dialect comes into your story, when it's natural for a character to speak in dialect, then you must convey this impression of dialect without tying your reader in knots and bringing him to a halt. The sense of the dialogue must continue to flow.

It isn't easy. In fact it's extremely difficult to convey dialect without bogging the reader down and slowing the pace of your story.

You can do it, firstly, by the carefull choice of NAMES. Never underestimate the importance of names your characters have. They can, and must, tell your reader much about your character.

SUBTLE IMPLICATION

Without giving the matter conscious thought, a reader will expect a character to speak with a strong Irish brogue if his name is Patrick O'Shea, and his home background a village in County Clare.So very carefully, with a word here and another there of easily understood dialect, and a clever twist of phrase - because everyone knows that the Irish usually put the cart before the darlin' horse in their manner of speaking - you'll convince your reader that your broth of a boy, Pat O'Shea, has a brogue could could cut with a knife.

Most of this enchanting game is done by implication, and with the lightest of delicate touches.

With the regional or national dialect of your own or any other lad, and where you have set your story, be subtle when introducing it into your stories.

How many of us, not London born and raised, would be able to make head or tail of cockney in the raw, when met on the printed page? Yet we can race at full tilt through the pages of books by Wolf Mankowitz, John Braine and others when their characters act out their stories in London surroundings.

Such writers have mastered this problem of dialect so that even the American or other unfamiliar reader can understand their essentially British city characters - London and the Midlands, Scotland, Wales and Ireland, all as distinctive as they can be.

You know that if your teenage character is shown behaving and dressed for the part, you have only to include such phrases into your dialogue as 'Hey, man, that's real groovey!', or 'Say, dig that bird! Ain't she summin again?', (I'm quite sure you could have come up with much more telling phrases!) for your readers to understand perfectly that your young character is a cockney 'mod'. You don't have to make the dialogue unintelligible to readers of a different generation to get your point across.

You may well be into this funky lingo far deeper than I am, so many any changes in the above that you think are meaningful, will you man? I just hope you dig me loud and clear.

The same applies to the sland and swearing of soldiers and sailors - among others! Although it's the fashion nowadays to use strong language with no holds barred, there really is no good purpose served by plastering your work with expressions that are raw and offensive - unless that's the kind of story you're writing. When it's up to you, naturally. I simply suggest that it's silly to use violence in word or action - if violence is out of place. I do know some writers who imagine the introduction of some crude language gives their stories strength. But it needs more than that surely?

We all know how one can form a vivid impression that a character is foul-mouthed and thoroughly unpleasant, by introducing a word here and there, and the reader will be convinced that your character's language is salty in the extreme... Give your reader's imagination a chance to fill in the picture.

As they say - it's all in the mind of the reader.

Think what Bernard Shaw did with the brilliantly placed single word 'Bloody' in *'Pygmalion'*. He didn't have to use a string of oaths. They wouldn't have been nearly so dramatic anyway. It was the placing, the timing, that was all-important.

Just as you have to use adjectives as though they were jewels, and never as sequins, so you have to use character-revealing words to the best possible effect.

You must be constantly building your charaters up in the minds of your readers through their behaviour, their appearance, their names - and their dialogue, including dialect.

Very often writers bewail, 'But I'm no earthly good at dialogue!'

They don't realise that it's something that has to be worked at consistently and forever if one makes writing one's life work. It isn't a knack one can pick up in an hour or two. And there isn't a magic formula for writing true-to-life dialogue.

CONVINCING DIALOGUE

I don't know any better way to learn how to write dialogue - convincing dialogue - than this. LISTEN TO THE THINGS PEOPLE SAY, AND THEIR WAYS OF SAYING THEM.

Study radio and television plays whenever possible. You should learn a lot that way. And don't forget to have your notebook and pen with you for making notes.

Read the kind of stories and novels you want to write. See how other writers have handled dialogue and dialect.

You must, of course, study the work of writers of other lands, but don't neglect your native writers, wherever you may live. There's sometimes a tendency to play down the writers of one's own country. I suppose it stems from that perfectly true saying, 'A prophet in his own land seldom gets the merit he deserves' - or words to that effect.

Wherever you were born, be quite sure there are writers you can be proud of among your fellow writers - and who can teach you a thing or two about your craft.

A STORY A DAY

Every short story writer should read a story a day as part of their regular routine.

And when I say 'Read a story', I mean analyse it, find out how the writer has overcome the various problems that are possibly your concern right now. Just skimming through stories can be of little real help. They have to be studied in detail, taken apart, read a second or even a third time if need be.

Regard every story and every novel you read, as a lesson to be thoroughly assimilated. Clearly understood. Make notes while you read. Think about every aspect of it. Imagine other ways in which you could develop the basic plot. Make the characters more alive.

DON'T NEGLECT USING THAT BRAIN OF YOURS. There's no limit to its potential.

And note who published the novel, or which magazine printed that story. Because Market Research must go hand in hand with your writing routine. You want to sell your work, don't you? So you must know the most likely markets to submit it to. As I mentioned before, different publishers specialise in different types of book.

You'll find that out quickly enough when your big, fat MSS start going the rounds. Many of the inevitable rejection slips will tell you that your beloved book 'doesn't fit into our list'. In other words - you've chosen the wrong publisher. And if this happens too often it will cost you a mint in postage, and waste a great deal of time. SO STUDY MARKETS. Find out who's publishing what - and make a note of it.

If you aren't certain of the categories of books a certain publisher handles, even after you've studied your *'Writers' and Artists' Yearbook'*, write and ask them for one of their recent catalogues. (It's as well to enclose a stamped, self-addressed envelope large enough for the catalogue.)

Study these catalogues carefully and file them.

Browse in bookshops and libraries whenever you have a spare hour. It will certainly repay you - as well as stretching those legs that have become cramped with too much desk-sitting before your hard-worked typewriter.

LET THEM TALK

Reverting to the very important subject of writing dialogue... One of the most common faults in writing dialogue is that it really is difficult to stand back and let the characters do the talking.

This is because one has become so closely involved with the work in hand - constructing the plot, thinking the characters into being, designing the whole scene and bringing it alive - that very often the dialogue becomes the author's, and not the characters', - and this won't do.

The only way to avoid it is to know your characters so well that they'll live their own independent lives - through you.

As you watch them in action you'll find them taking over from you and writing their own dialogue, refusing to say anything thats uncharacteristic.

So much can be put across across to the reader in a few lines of dialogue. For instance, G.B.Stern wrote this in the story, *'The Slower Judas'* :

'Cliffe? Let me see, are you the Cliffe who wrote *'The Devil A Monk Would Be?'*

'No. That was my father.'

'Your father? Oh yes! Then you must be the Cliffe who wrote that wonderful ironic thing - a poem, wasn't it? - *'Not At Home To Hannibal?'*

'No. That was my son.'

There you have a wraith of a man almost squeezed to death, it would seem, between two literary giants - his father and his son.

You notice the economy of writing? No 'He said', 'She said'. Just dialogue revealing the questioner, an eater of literary lions, hungry for a meal. And the man who is only too aware of the fact that he couldn't even provide an appetizer.

* * * * *

If you have any doubts about your dialogue, if you fear it may be stilted, then read it aloud to yourself - but always with the character who is speaking clearly in mind.

KNOW THE RULES - THEN BREAK THEM.

I want to say something here about Punctuation and Sentence Length. And I want you to think about what I'm going to tell you.

Of course you may agree, or disagree. What matters is that you think about it and come to your own conclusions.

Punctuation is a personal matter. But you have to know the rules before you can break them. They may only be broken for very good reasons. That goes for all the other rules as well. The rules of Grammar included.

You may consider the stories and novels of Hemingway too old hat to be considered. It's your loss if you do. Like Guy de Maupassant, and others who have shaped our literature, Hemingway wrote the way he did for a very good reason.

He was reflecting his time.

Some writers have read Hemingway's staccato sentences, and have formed the idea that all they have to do if they would emulate him, is to scatter full stops like confetti, and the result will be the same. How can they do wrong? He did it and got away with it, didn't he?

Believe me, Hemingway had good reason for placing every punctuation mark exactly where he did. When you study the stories he left - and it will pay you to study them periodically - try to understand just how clever he was in this. What his reasons were for rattling out dialogue like machine-gun fire.

THE REASON WAS THAT HE WAS WRITING ABOUT THE BLOOD AND AGONY AND THE DRAMA OF THE

BATTLEFIELD AND BULLRING, AND HIS METHOD OF WRITING HEIGHTENED THE TENSION AS NO OTHER TECHNIQUE COULD HAVE DONE.

Very briefly, this is what one should remember...

It is that short, sharp sentences and paragraphs - whether dialogue or descriptive - convey tension, or humour, or high drama. You're punching away against the clock.

You can't imagine writing - or reading - long, leisurely, sweet-sailing prose describing war, or a hurricane, or panic in the streets, can you?

THE IMPORTANCE OF RHYTHM

There must be rhythm in everything we write. There must be a purpose for writing the way we do. In the shape and sound of the words we use, as well as in the meaning. In the way we cut and frame our words, our thoughts, our action.

General Smuts called it 'The Oneness of Life.' The association and interdependence of every large and small thing, one with the other. The Poetry Of Life, if you like.

Don't strain after effect. It won't work that way. Let your effects build up in your mind and flow naturally at their proper pace. Be yourself in everything you write. Don't waste time and effort trying to copy other writers, and in cultivating gimmicks. It never works.

Every writer is unique in his own way. And it's just that quality of uniqueness that we must foster and contribute to life. Not as something 'precious' - in the sense that it's affected - but as something natural.

Reverting to the subject of Grammar, listen to what Professor Randolph Quirk has to say. He is professor of modern

English at London University. This should cheer you considerably - I hope.

'Why on earth shouldn't you end a sentence with a preposition' he demands? 'That sort of thing leads to pretentious people saying, 'To whom do you wish to speak?' when you mean, 'Who do you want to talk to?' To say that one thing is right in grammar and that another thing is wrong - as if grammar is a form of morality - is a practice I have no patience with. There's no such thing as 'pure' in English. The thing is to talk like the people you live with.'

And that goes for the people you write about, too. Make them live in everything they do, and in what they say, and you'll be on the right lines.

* * * * *

So bear in mind when writing dialogue that its functions are these:

1. It should be *in character* - which means that it should not be in *your* character.

2. It should *reveal character*.

3. It should bring the setting to ife, and build up *atmosphere* and *mood*.

4. It should carry the *action* forward.

5. It must *never be used as padding*. Your characters must never waffle. Remember - DIALOGUE IS THE CONDENSED ESSENCE OF THE SPOKEN WORD. The likeness to actual speech is an illusion. Fiction-speech must be artificially created with the characters who are speaking kept vividly and firmly in mind.

If you read such magazines as *Woman's Journal*, *Cosmopolitan* and *She*, you'll know the stories of Audrey Curling. She's one of the most successful and prolific story-writers in Britain today.

She has some sound advice for those would-be writers who mourn the fact that a full time job, or a home and children, cuts writing time down to nil and makes professional story-writing impossible.

Audrey Curling has a job, runs a home, and writes professionally as well. And she's only human.

For years she's made a habit of reading at least one short story a day, analysing it automatically in her brain as she reads, and she prefers the stories of the late Somerset Maugham to those of any other writer in this category because 'He achieves his effect with such a beautiful economy of words'

How does she fulfil her obligations and write as much as she does?

She says it's by giving thought to her stories as she waits for buses, strap-hangs, does the shopping, or cooks the dinner.

Then, she says, 'I write in the evening, and I find my output rises when I have a job. When I'm at home all day with plenty of time to write I find I tend to put things off, but with a full time job every minute of free time is precious.'

Many writers find the same thing. The secret of becoming a full time professional writer is self-discipline. Without it, one never gets off the ground.

Gear yourself to writing at a good fast pace, however much or however little time you can devote to writing.It's usually more stimulating than slow-paced work. And slow writers often find to their distress that they run the risk of grinding to a halt. It's so fatally easy to lapse into a day-dream or have one's thoughts wander to other things, if the mind isn't firmly held in check. Your interest must be rivetted.

For this reason I've known several writers who work with their backs to the window to avoid distraction. It's sensible to realise our weaknesses and temptations, and take steps to keep our noses to the grindstone.

To return to Audrey Curling, here is the sound advice she gives to beginners in short story writing:

'Never rush at a piece of work. A worth while short story is not something that can be tossed off in the course of an evening. If you have an idea that seems good to you, keep it at the back of your mind and think about it from all possible angles, for weeks if necessary, before you actually write it.

'If you feel you must make a rough draft, do so, but put it away for a time, and if it still looks good when you take it out again, it's probably worth writing up. That isn't to say that a writer should indulge in long fallow periods while a story shapes itself.

'THE JOB OF A WRITER IS TO WRITE SOMETHING EVERY DAY.'

There you have it said once again. There must be something in it, mustn't there?

And this is what Marie Oxenford wrote about Audrey Curling after she had interviewed her..

'As I chatted with Audrey Curling I realised that the reason for her success is the meticulous care that goes into every piece of work she submits to an editor, and the infinite trouble she takes to make sure that every story goes to the right market.'

There you have it - in a nutshell!

You won't find it easy to write something every day. None of us do to begin with. But it really is the only way to forge yourself into a writer. And I promise you, if you stick at it and do your daily writing stint, it will in time flow easily and will bring all kinds of tangible and intangible rewards. All in good time - but inevitably.

You know the saying, 'If you want something done, go to a busy person.'

It has to do with Tempo - mental and physical. Our minds and our bodies become geared to Slow, Medium and Fast. And, believe me, because one is working slowly, it's no sort of criterion that one is working well. Usually quite the reverse. A full, demanding life is far more stimulating than an empty one - I don't need to tell you that. I often think the amount of time some would-be writers spend lamenting lack of time, simply shows that they're either badly adjusted mentally and physically, or that they have the wrong outlook on life. That they're negative and self-destructive.

We should sing for joy when we're surging along at full pressure - just as we do when we're jurtling along an open road at speed. It should exhilarate us. Bring out our best. Instead of which I often find people who bitterly resent having to extend themselves to meet life's demands.

CHAPTER SEVEN

METHODS OF WRITING, EMOTIONAL SCENES.

Let us begin this chapter by clearing up a few of the misconceptions and problems that often trouble new writers. It's absolutely necessary that we thoroughly understand and master each step we take in our progress towards professional writing.

I presume that you're actually writing stories at this point, and sending them out hopefully to chosen markets.

You must be your own sternest critic. If your work doesn't measure up to what you appreciate is the standard expected by editors, then you must take immediate steps to improve it. That makes sense, doesn't it?

Bear in mind that you're competing from your first submitted manuscript with experienced professional writers, in whatever field you've chosen to work in - presumably, at this point, short stories. And you're sufficiently handicapped already by lack of experience, without adding to your difficulties.

But don't lose heart. Every writer was a beginner at one time. And there's no reason on earth why you shouldn't make a giant leap into professional writing - if you've the will to!

It simply doesn't make sense to exclude slip-shod appearance of MSS by saying that you're not a professional typist. Or to admit that you know you're weak in spelling, grammar or punctuation, or that surely these are minor matters when compared with the fact that you're turning out jolly good stories - if you do say so yourself!

I've known would-be writers persistently shrug off the importance of professionalism in their work on the assumption that it's an editor's job to see that spelling, grammatical and punctuation mistakes are put right. ‘What are sub-editors for?’ they say.

Of course they're entirely wrong. Every aspect of your finished manuscript IS YOUR JOB, and you're failing at the outset if you send out work that isn't beyond reproach in appearance at least.

BE PROFESSIONAL.

You see, the whole question goes much deeper than the surface. All the time we should be building up our standards, developing our integrity and expertise as writers.

You know what appears to be happening not only in our country, but in the world at large through an apparent general lowering of technical standards.

You complain that you can't read the paper without coming across careless mistakes in sentence construction, in news presentation, in spelling, statistics, and grammar. Those typographical mistakes irritate you; those badly captioned pictures blunt the point of the picture strip, or raise a question in your mind.

Each of these familiar mistakes is the fault of some individual concerned with the paper's production, who has this deplorable lax attitude to this work, which we're considering. The ‘What the hell - ?’ frame of mind.

Never let us fall below our own high standards. We must check and double-check our work before sending it out. It will be the quickest and the surest route to success in the long run.

I've found that reading a story aloud on the second or third revision is an excellent plan. The ear often picks up a mistake that the eye has passed.

This is what a very experienced short story writer, Beatrice Levin, wrote on the subject of revision:

'Learning to do constructive, intelligent revision is one of the hardest lessons any writer must accomplish. The difference between 're-typing' and 're-writing' is the same as the difference between worrying and planning.

'In worrying you cover the same ground over and over without going forward, gnawing at the problem without coming to any real decision about it.

'But in attacking a problem realistically, with the intent of doing something to settle or solve it, you are planning. In the same way, if you take a manuscript and merely set out to re-type it, changing a word here, omitting a paragraph there, or adding a clearly sharpened word, you aren't really taking a giant step forward. In fact, you aren't tackling your problem at all.'

When a story has been rejected a couple of times, or when you're not satisfied with the way a MSS reads or looks, you simply must give it your full concentration.

You must give your story a new look, and if necessary re-write it without compromise.

Our stories are often so near and dear to us - an affection and confidence built up over hours of hard work and much thought - that we're very reluctant to rip them apart at the seams when they've proved unsaleable, and create an entirely new garment from the pieces. But we must often be ruthless to be realistic.

I've schooled myself over many tough years of writing to grasp the nettle when instinct - or editors - tell me that there's something wrong with a story.

I give it the whole works. 'This time it will be better!' I tell myself. 'This time the thing will sell - or I'll bury it in a drawer and forget it!' And believe me I turn my whole concentration on it, working at it until I know I can't improve it. If I'm not satisfied, how can I expect an editor to be?

MEN IN A WOMAN'S WORLD.

Women sometimes express their surprise when they learn that the editors of at least two of Britain's most successful 'Women's Magazines' are men. In fact I've heard some resentful comments from certain quarters.

But the fact remains that these men would certainly not have been given their editorial chairs unless the shrewd old powers that be had been certain that they were the best talent money could buy.

No one achieves this kind of status except on merit. They've had to prove themselves every step up the highly competitive, difficult ladder. And surely it's sexist - today's ugly word - to imagine otherwise.

It's really just another sign of the changing times, and one to applaud. Most certainly the standard of our magazines has risen in recent years. In every department, the realism and the quality of writing of our serials and stories; the depth of field and the unblinking range of subjects tackled in the features and editorials; the quality of our illustrations - think how they've all improved over the past ten years.

On the whole the range of magazines now on sale around the world is excellent, and contributors have to face steep competition and an increasing challenge.

I know several story writers who were very successful la few years ago, who've become bitter and defeatist because of their inability to compete with magazine story writers today.

Some - the silly or deluded ones - blame decline in literary quality and taste or inefficient editors who 'don't recognise a good story when they see one', as a writer complained the other day. After all, fashions in clothes have changed, haven't they? But they're not falling behind yesterday's. It's just that they're different - and they're what people want.

It's really a very insular point of view, isn't it? We should look about us and ask the question, 'What HASN'T changed in the last decade?' Just about everything has, and if we're not to be left behind, dreaming of past successes and giving up the struggle in advance, we'd better take careful stock of the world about us, of the magazines and other markets prepared to consider our work - if it's good enough! - and we must be prepared to change with the changing times. IF WE CAN. We's be the losers if we don't.

For instance, it's no good decrying the changes that have come about in the structure and the problems of family life. I'm sure many of us do. But, as writers, we must try to undersand the pressures that threaten families today, as well as the kind of fiction read by parents and young people living in today's society.

We must write ABOUT society today. And we must write FOR today's society. What on earth is the good of writing at all otherwise?

The world's an exciting, demanding place today. There has never been a greater challenge on every front. It isn't all doom and gloom by any means. It may seem sometimes that some of the young freak out in appearance and public behaviour, and older folk may appear to take a dim view of their youngsters' antics, but how much is bravado on the one hand, lack of communication and understanding on the other?

People are still reading stories - thank God! They still want well written stories about love and courage, frustration and heartbreak; funny stories, sad stories, stories of hope and achievement. And most of all the readers of magazines demand love stories, because that's as real and as potent today as ever it was.

But don't put blinkers on. Look about you. Try to understand what's going on. And write stories that are in tune with today.

Take a tip from our home decorators and dress designers, many of them men of course, and see how they've interpreted the mood and the need of the moment in the colours, styles and accessories they've chosen to fit the changing attitude of society today.

The only thing wrong with change is not keeping pace with it. And that's up to us.

TABOOS

And that brings us to the question of taboos.

Not so long ago we writers had to read very warily in the minefield of taboos which society planted around us. There were all manner of subjects that were forbidden ground.

We didn't dare write about mental illness, drugs, homosexuality, politics, or any of the other sober subjects or experiences that faced adults in everyday life - unless they were among the fortunate minority. Death, and even divorce were unacceptable subjects with most publishers and editors. There was a very rigid code indeed.

I remember receiving a long, explicit letter from an editor not so long ago, explaining why she couldn't use a story I'd written with death as the theme. To me it was a perfectly straightforward story in which death played a natural and inevitable part.

But she explained that, as far as her magazine was concerned - it was one of the more serious monthlies - all mention of death was OUT - unless it was the gentle, perfectly natural death of someone of advanced age, and then preferably one whose Will was going to transform the lives of the hero or heroine from want to plenty. Then the ancient soul was allowed to pass on - but only in a few carefully chosen sentences. Nothing that would be likely to depress or distress the reader.

Thankfully this is no longer the usual attitude of those in editorial chairs. I guess it must be getting through to them that nowadays, with Life the funny old business it often is, Death can have its appeal. It's no longer the bogeyman to end all bogeymen.

There are still taboos of course. I expect there always will be, but they're getting fewer every year. Much of it has to do with editors' prejudices, and you can easily find out what they are by studying the stories appearing in their journals.

This is one of the many aspects of story writing that is, as they say, on-going. Which means that you have to keep pace with market changes, as with the taste of the reading public.

The wise writer keeps a finger on the pulse of the great, complex, ever-changing magazine market to check its heart-beat.

The only possible way to do this is by regular market research. Ask yourself a few straight questions, such as:

1. How many possible new markets have you found recently?

2. What changes in policy or editorial management have you noticed in your favourite magazines in the past few months?

3. How do my rejected stories differ from those published in recent issues of the magazines I study?

4. Am I confident that I'm maintaining my highest standards? If not, why?

EMOTIONS, AND HOW TO HANDLE THEM.

Do you experience any special problems in writing about the emotional scenes that crop up in your stories? Many writers do.

Although magazine stories are more realistic and sophisticated than they were a few years ago, that doesn't mean that the emotions of your characters aren't as real and difficult to handle as ever they were. Probably more so, because they've come out in the open increasingly.

I was talking about stories for womens' magazines, and she said, 'I couldn't possibly write slush!'

She couldn't understand it when I said, 'Thank goodness for that, because there's precious little slush in any well written love story. Editors - and readers - would very quickly reject it.'

If you feel you're writing sentimental nonsense - that your love scenes are being written tongue in cheek, and that you're 'writing down", call a halt. You'll never succeed that way.

This mistaken idea that one can write sentimental rubbish for today's womens' magazines and get away with it spells failure from the outset. No writer would get away with it. You have to write from the heart as well as the head. Bear that in mind.

Love isn't sentimental nonsense. And it isn't just another word for 'sex'. Love is the very heart of the matter, to be treated with due respect - which doesn't mean that it can't be funny, tender, revealing and transforming, and the most fundamental emotion of all.

Just how you're going to express emotional scenes in your stories - the whole range of emotions, I mean, not excluding the emotion of Love - is something that can only be learned through study and practice. Each of us evolves our own forms of expression.

But it's essential that you study the markets you're trying to enter - study them individually, making mental and written notes of your findings for future guidance.

Learn how the successful writers whose work appears in these magazines express such emotions as Fear, Loneliness, Loss, Grief, Rejoicing, Heartbreak, Joy or Loving.

You'll find that each type of magazine favours its own methods of expression. Some are subtle and clever, others naive, or blunt, or revealing in their depth, while others are sophisticated, or inhibited, in keeping with the kind of characters acting out their lives in the stories favoured by individual magazines.

You'll find that emotion can be conveyed in many different ways. It must be shown in the behaviour of your characters - in small things such as the way a door is opened or closed, a curtain drawn, a child corrected or consoled.

Dialogue can disclose so much more than the actual words say. And the kind of emotion can be dramatically heightened by the physical setting of your story, so that it all builds up into a comprehensible whole.

For instance, it isn't only on radio or television that emotional scenes are deliberately played out against such accompanying natural drama as gathering storms, rough seas, a high wind or blizzard.

It can be very effective to play your emotional scene in harmony with the drama of Nature. But it must be handled in subtle, clever ways.

You can work wonders by the sensitive use of background accompaniment to the tears and tempers, the fighting, laughter and loving of your characters. They don't exist in a void. So draw in the surrounding scene cleverly, depending on the interplay of characters, action, mood and nature.

You wouldn't expect high drama against a flute-sweet symphony of doves, bees, and the distant voices of happy children, would you?

In spite of which there are times when you can use just such sharp contrast to accent the emotional chords being struck by your key characters. It can be like splashing crimson across a mist-grey background. They call it using shock tactics in presenting emotional conflict, and it can be most effective if properly handled.

So you see, you can either play your emotional scenes low and sweet - a loving young couple making ends meet in a country cottage or a city flat, the climax of the story no more than a tender-comic little storm in a breakfast cup to do with neighbours, parents-in-law, bills, babies, or whether or not they should plant a rose-bush in the centre of their tiny lawn....In other words, it can arise from any of the minor emotional experiences we all have to face and solve in life.

Or it can be one of the major experiences that scar the heart, or wreck lives, or save them, or sweep obstacles, landmarks, loved ones away, to be lost in the ocean of life.

You can't give such a variety of emotions the same treatment, can you? That's where the poet in you takes over. And never forget that there's a poet in every one of us, just as there's breath in every living body.

YOU ARE A POET.

Many writers hotly deny that they have any poetry in their make-up. But I've found that, given the right circumstances, they will probably surprise themselves.

Think about your particular problem of the moment - which is, of course, the problem involving your characters. And then see how your characters, and their immediate problem, are being affected by surrounding circumstances. How large and small things affect the situation in which you have placed them.

Sum everything up, and then bring it all in to work its collective magic. If you play your hand right, you'll find that the right atmosphere has been created to give your story wings.

Realism is so much more than down-to-earth, prosaic facts of life.

Even in the most realistic stories you can do so much by introducing some of the symbolism of Nature, for instance. For, wherever our story is located, the natural setting can never be ignored. And it is always there, waiting to be drawn into the action, and to breathe the poetry of life into it.

You can't help but be aware of the bursting buds of spring, for instance, heightening the sense of joy, young love, optimism and renewed faith.

Or the nostalgic ache the falling leaves of autumn bring by association.

Then the high noon of summer, when life is comparatively rip-roaring, with little thought of the drawn of the day, or the twilight yet to come.

And the evening of winter, when people are gently shut within doors and made to face themselves and each other.

We can't escape the symbolism of Nature when creating our stories.

So let Nature help you solve your emotional problems as you write. And appreciate what a help it can be if we read the poets, and the masters of prose. If we listen to good music, mood music, emotional music, while we think about the emotional problems our characters are facing. It can be of help and inspiration to us.

Just a word about endearments, because this can be a problem - in a literary sense.

Use them sparingly, and place them with the greatest care. You know how the word 'darling' loses all meaning when anyone scatters the word like currants in an old-fashioned bun.

Three characters have just popped into my mind, unbidden, all of them saying the same word, 'Ducks'. One is a London Clippie - 'Shove along, Ducks!' The next a shy professor who suddenly bends down in a corridor and whispers in a pretty student's ear - 'Ullo - er - Ducks!' which electrifies them both. And the third, an old estranged couple, who go silently to the moves, purely from habit, each of them nursing a terrible burden of bitterness towards the other. And then a community song strikes up, 'My Old Dutch!'. And when it's over the old man digs into his pocket for a bag of peppermints and whispers, 'Ave one, Ducks!'

You see what I mean? One word of endearment, with three very different shades of meaning.

STORE YOUR EMOTIONS.

I remember a well-known novelist confessing, with surprise and a little shame in her voice;

'It really horrified me to find that I was studying my reactions with detached fascination, at my husband's funeral. It's been the same in all my most difficult and heart-breakking moments, and it's something I can't prevent myself doing. It's as though the writer in me stands apart and takes close, impersonal note of all my most deeply felt emotional experiences.'

And she wasn't alone. Many writers have spoken of a similar inability to cast off the writer who has taken over so much of their lives, and react as a private, solitary person.

Is this something one should feel ashamed about? I don't think so. How best can we understand and portray emotions if we don't learn all we can from our own personal emotions?

I think it was Somerset Maugham who wrote a story about a man who met his downfall because of his inability to let some of his most compromising relationships and reactions go unrecorded. What he most deeply felt, he wrote down. And in the end his diaries revealed the secrets of his outwardly blameless life, as diaries have had an uncomfortable habit of doing through the years.

I can't think of a better, more helpful way of writing about the emotions of our characters, than through personal experience. But writers must be discreet, however difficult it may be.

That remarkably fine Irish novelist and story writer, Edna O'Brien, told us during a television interview not long ago that the reason why she lives in London, rather than her beloved Ireland, was because she couldn't help bringing her emotional experiences from the past, and her friends from childhood, into her writing. They walked right out of her memory onto the written sheet. And the people of her home town couldn't forgive her.

'How can a writer know about emotions other than through the lessons life has taught?' she asked. 'And it isn't possible for one to be sure how much one is revealing through one's characters. They take over and draw from one's past, often without one being aware of the fact. Imagination and memory play a very subtle game, you know!'

HEADY EXPERIENCE.

Writing stories isn't just an exercise in creative writing. It's much more than that.

It means holding a firm grip on the reins where your aharacters are concerned. Never giving them their head and letting them run off with the story - and with your good sense.

It happens so often, at times to the complete surprise of the writer, who has created a character - and that character grows and grows in strength and independence, becoming ever more forcibly alive. And, before the writer knows it, the plot he has formed so carefully is trampled underfoot by the rampaging creature he has let loose in the garden of his mind.

It's a wonderful heady feeling for a writer to experience. It's like riding a strong horse and having the brute suddenly take control out of your hands and go thundering across country while you hang on for dear life - thrilled, terrified, apprehensive, and inwardly shouting for joy.

The trouble is that it feels like inspiration. The writer often imagines that he's writing powerful stuff. But, if you cast your mind back, isn't that exactly how certain run-away, exciting dreams felt before you awoke to the reality that - they didn't make sense. They made *non*sense?

What sometimes seems like crystal clear, inspired thinking, between sleeping and waking, crumbles into dust when recalled in the harsh light of day.

So beware of being taken for a thrilling ride by your characters. Just keep a firm grip on the reins, and control the pace and direction.

CHAPTER EIGHT

INTRODUCING THE NOVEL.

Of course much of what we have studied concerning short story writing applies to novel-writing. In the same way painting miniatures and murals may be said to have many laws of technique that are similar.

Many writers of short stories find that their interest naturally extends to tackling the writing of novels. They begin by writing a short story or two, and then find that the subject they have conceived and planned begins to develop beyond the circumscribed limits of the short story, and demands space to grow into a novel. Their characters and action demand the freedom to expand.

They say that everyone has at least one good book in them. My experience backs this theory. I've known the most unlikely men and women to produce books that have been published, and, most importantly, have brought the writers fulfilment. Some have opened the door to a new life of achievement and security beyond their early dreams. Very many first novels have drawn strongly on autobiographical material, which is to be expected.

Once you have given expression to the imagination that may have haunted you with day-dreams for years, and you begin to write - there's really no knowing where it will lead you!

So in this introduction to novel-writing I hope you will be helped take a brave step forward.

What others have done - you can do! Never doubt it.

Let me start by asking you a personal question. Perhaps several. Only you and I need know the answers.

Why do you want to write? Is it for fulfilment, because you feel you have to write - or bust?

Is it simply that you hope to make money this way?

Or are your eyes raised to the small, shining ranks of the famous, the writers who have won prestigious literary awards and honours, and fat, fat, cheques?

This is make-up-your-mind time, so give it a thought. And be honest. You need to know at the outset where you're trying to go, and how to steer for your goal, whatever it may be. You need to understand what motivated you, and how much you want to succeed.

THE VARIOUS KINDS OF NOVEL.

Just as there are a number of different categories of novel, so there are many ways of writing a novel. So don't expect me to lay down anything more explicit than suggestions and guidelines, and some heart-felt warnings, gleaned from experience. My experience, but much more, the experience of other writers who really have achieved success in whatever field they have tackled.

Some successful novelists begin with no more than an opening paragraph or two, and a hazy idea about the plot and characters that are building up in their minds. As one novelist explained it: 'They evolve and take over to tell the story in their own way, with practically no help from me at all - apart from getting it down on paper.'

This seems quite extraordinary to me, for I can't imagine writing a book being other than hard, sustained work.

'How do I know how my novel's going to end?' I heard an author say recently to an awestruck audience. 'It hasn't written itself yet, has it? I just hand the thing over and let it roll!'

Well, I admit near the end of a long, hard buffetting in the seas of life, I can only react in disbelief, or shall we say, astonishment, to statements like that.

By far the greater number of writers I know, or whose autobiographies I have read, are meticulous craftsmen who accept full responsiblity for their work from first to last, with no nonsense about inspiration 'taking them over.'

Some of them, I'd say the majority, refrain from writing a word of the actual text until the whole elaborate scaffolding has gone up from page one to the end.

At times there seem to be no limits to which these conscientious grafters won't go. They research for days, weeks, months, sometimes for years on a single novel, gathering historical, geographical and other material.

It's quite possible that they find they must travel extensively, painstakingly interviewing, making endless notes, sometimes photographing or sketching actual or possible settings.

I've known some authors who find it suseful to work with a separate large manilla envelope or folder for each carefully planned chapter of a book.

On the outside of each folder they write details of the unfolding action, pen-pictures of the characters featuring in the action of that chapter, and scraps of dialogue important to the plot. Just as small-scale models are very often made of each scene in a stage or screen play for the director's guidance.

They evolve all kinds of personal techniques to help them along, for I repeat that every novelist is a law unto himself in their manner of working.

Sometimes they will even cut out pictures of people, places and props from magazines, to add to these individual chapter-folders. And I know one very experienced novelist who pins pictures of his characters and settings to small peg-boards, which stand before him on his desk to keep them clearly in mind as he works.

He explains that he finds this particularly helpful because he usually has to work on several very different assignments simultaneously.

Whatever the differences of the working plans of these writers have been, I've never known even a moderately successful novelist who hasn't given serious thought, and done a lot of preliminary work, before tackling a book.

I don't doubt that you've heard people say that they write 'purely by inspiration', as though God had taken over. And that they bash out their books from start to finish on their machines with practically no forethoughts, planning or research, and still less revision or re-writing.

There's no real harm in this kind of fantasising - UNLESS IT'S BELIEVED!

It's when someone with literary ambitions falls for this kind of fairy tale, and tries to write in this painless way himself, inevitably finding that he can't follow along that easy road, that the trouble lies.

It's quite possible, in such circumstances, that he'll lose confidence in himself, despair, and even give up writing altogether. THAT'S WHERE THE DANGER LIES.

To avoid this pitfall, I suggest that you brush up your sense of humour, take large pinches of salt, and recognise these phoney stories of novels that write themselves, for what they are. Don't be cruel and ask such leading questions as whether these novels that have written themselves have ever been published. It could lead to embarrassment.

I'm sure that such fantasies would never be voiced by serious writers whose books appear in shops and reviews. Hard experience has taught them better.

Dorothea Brande asked her students at the opening session of every course she held on Creative Writing:

'Are you prepared to work hard? And I mean HARD?'

And she would impress on them,'If you aren't, forget all about becoming a writer. You've failed before you start.'

YOUR KIND OF NOVEL.

Don't dive into the deep end and begin to plan a novel until you've given it hard thought and decided on the kind of novel you really want to write. The kind you'll feel at ease with. The kind you desperately want to write. The kind you prefer to read, and with which you're familiar.

The range is wide and varied. There are thrillers, romances, murder mysteries, books about war and discovery and high adventure; there are all kinds of historical novels and biographies, science fiction, steamy novels about sex and violence, and long, thick family sagas. The list's pretty well endless.

The important thing is to know what you're writing about.

In other words - *write about what you know, and what really interests you.*

In the beginning at any rate, don't attempt to write about people, places or problems that are unfamiliar to you. You need to build up your self-confidence and expertise as a novelist first, and writing about unfamiliar things demands much research.

Four things are essential no matter what kind of novel you write.

The theme and tone of your novel should have immediacy. It should slot into the mood that prevails around you at this moment in history.

Ask yourself what people are reading and thinking, what they're concerned with domestically, nationally, and even internationally - what the news media is feeding into their lives day after day after day? What do they need for distraction? And be guided by these factors if possible.

You must bring Thought, Emotion and Action into your novels. And your characters must be convincing, they must come alive for your readers.

Bear in mind that enthusiasm is the most valuable ingredient of any writer's outfit. Without it your work will be flat and boring, and your own zest for the hard work involved in writing a novel will cool down. Perhaps peter out altogether. Enthusiasm is the very breath of life to your creative work. Never forget that.

STAYING POWER.

Next on the list of basic essentials, I'd say, if you're determined to become a successful author, is staying power. The sheer determination to carry on. Never to admit defeat.

Here is a famous novelist's frank admission and advice which may inspire you.

Novelist Barbara Taylor Bradford, whose books half the world seems to be reading these days, tells us that she scrapped her first four novels when she'd written about a hundred pages.

She'd known from early childhood that she wanted nothing more than to be a novelist, and, after selling many short stories, and working successfully for some years as a journalist, she really believed all she had to do was to sit herself down and write her first novel. She saw no obstacles whatever. It would be a piece of cake.

'It didn't occur to me that I'd strike any snags, she said in a recent interview. 'I knew I could write. I'd served my apprenticeship in several fields of writing. And I'd succeeded in everything I'd tried.

'Now, when I felt myself ready to begin my career as a novelist, surely all I had to do was to have a good idea, sit down at my desk, and write it.

'But it didn't work out like that at all. The wonderful ideas I kept having for novels simply ran out after a hundred pages or so. I dried up. It was mortifying.

'It took me some time and much agonising before I realised that a novel mmust be planned and carefully structured.'

She pointed out that a house isn't built without much planning, surveying, gathering together of the various building materials. And then must come the hard work of construction *according to plan.* Writing a novel, she discovered, has much in common with building a house.

When at last she faced her apparent failure as a novelist and realised that it wasn't her writing ability that had let her down, but her manner of tackling an entirely new technique, Barbara Taylor Bradford set to work again.

'I asked myself a few important questions,' she said. 'Such as where did I want to place my novel and in what period of time. Although I was living mostly in America at that time, my husband being a film director, I realised that I was still and always would be a Yorkshire lass at heart. And it was about my native Yorkshire and my roots that I must write my first important novel.

'I had always been an ambitious, capable and hard-working person, so it was natural that my first key character, Emma, should be a woman of my own kind. One I could thoroughly understand and relate to.'

It took her nearly two years to think, plan and write *'A Woman of Substance'* - and it achieved all and more than this writer had hoped for. It has brought her a large and ever-increasing fortune as run-away best-seller all over the world, from film and television and radio rights, foreign rights, and from subsequent contracts and advances for further blockbusters to follow.

'I still take about a year and a half to write a novel, and work from ten to twelve hours a day on my books because I'm a workaholic,' she says. 'I have no children and no family other than my husband, who is also devoted to his work.

'I would never dream of starting a book without a detailed story-line to guide me. Or write about people or places that meant little to me. Sometimes I rewrite a page up to ten times before it satisfies me.

'And I say quite categorically that anyone who says that they don't revise or rewrite a novel is either a hack or a liar!

Which is an opinion worth thinking about when one considers the hard experience and success behind it. This author writes about what she knows!

MUM'S THE WORD

In whatever way you decide to write your novel, and whichever kind of novel you want to tackle, there's one thing about which I must warn you very seriously indeed.

Keep it to yourself until it's done. Don't talk about it. Don't let anyone else read what you've written until the words 'THE END' have been typed, and you've cut the umbilical cord.

Creating a novel is a most private experience. And things can so easily go wrong.

The similarities between a book and a baby will amaze you when your time has come to reproduce yourself. From the first seed of thought, through all the months of gestation while it's developing inside you, it will be an intensely personal matter, not to be shared. You must brood over it, love and dream about it as the endless time goes by. It will feel like living a life within a life, believeme.

Do take this warning seriously - I have painful memories of how I once talked a most promising novel out of my system.

I'd spent weeks of intense mental activity, thinking, researching, making notes, gathering material. I was full to the brim with my beautiful, beloved novel. The characters had taken me over. I was possessed and could think of nothing else. And I'd been shut up with it all alone, for too long, working white hot, and not sleeping very much. Which is my way of working.

If only I hadn't gone out that morning! If only I'd taken a cold shower and made myself sleep for some hours, which I badly needed.

But instead I went shopping, for my cupboard was bare. I was obsessed by my book, seeing my characters instead of the people I met in the street; hearing their voices in my head.

I met a dear, patient friend outside a shop. She asked me what I was working on, why she hadn't seen me for a while? It triggered me off and the flood took over.

As she gradually wilted against the shop window I told her - everything! I watched myself in horror, helpless, as I bled my book to death. Once it started it was beyond my control - it all poured out.

I knew my book was lifeless before I sat down again in my study and looked squarely at what I had done. There wasn't a spark of life left in it. It meant nothing any more.

Oh, I tried to breathe life back into it, to revive the precious body, but to no purpose. Everything I'd written I packed into a case, and years later I destroyed it. I can hardly bear to think of the idiotic crime even now, many years later.

So I beg you, take my warning seriously. Your family and friends will be relieved. But of far greater importance, your brain child will have a sporting chance to mature inside you until it's whole and strong and beautiful, and ready to make a proper entry into the world.

You must have heard authors warn you many times that 'writing is an intensely solitary occupation'.

Believe me, it is. Prepare yourself to cope with it.

GET IT DOWN!

That most successful writer, Francis King, would like every writer new to the game to listen to his words of warning.

'I wish I could persuade new writers to listen to what I say - and ignore what I *do*,' he said. 'In one respect at least.'

He thinks about a book for about eighteen months, while he's milling out radio plays, stories, reviews and articles. The bills must be paid. But the trouble is that he doesn't write any of it down.

'Several times this habit of mine has resulted in disaster,' he says ruefully. 'I've been involved for too long in writing that has made great demands on my thought and time, and the novel that's been gestating in my mind for so long - evaporates!

'Suddenly I find that I've time to devote to getting the novel down on paper. I've completed whatever I was busy with - a collection of stories or a travel book, shall we say.

'I've cleared my desk and sat down to enjoy writing the novel I've put so much thought into. And I've been faced with a mental blank! The carefully structured novel has fragmented in my brain, and escaped. And because I haven't committed a word of it to paper, well, I find there's nothing there.

'This happened again recently. It seems I never learn! All I can hope is that some time the novel will all come back to mind, the time will be right, and I'll capture it again.'

Francis King has written a number of very successful novels, but they're quite different from one another. He has a horror of being type-cast, and enjoys the challenge of trying his hand at work of great variety.

'The Fire Walkers' is' as he says, 'a joyful book set in Greece, 'and it has recently been republished. There have been serious novels, thrillers, biographical novels from this versatile author, and he says that he has no idea what he will try his hand at next. Variety is his spice of life.

'In one way this is fine, 'he says. 'I certainly enjoy the variety. But it does mean that readers can be disappointed when they find that the humorous novel they enjoyed is followed by the kind that turns them off. They don't know what they can expect from me, and that isn't always a good thing.'

Of one thing he is quite sure. Writers should commit the story-line and characters to paper when a novel first takes shape in their minds, and not risk losing it by caging it in their heads without taking the precaution of making notes that will lead to its recapture if it escapes. GET IT DOWN!

CHAPTER NINE

AND SO TO WORK.

So you've decided on the kind of novel you intend to write

You must now decide on the setting and period - the place and time.

Having carefully chosen all this, settle down with it and be aware of it with all your senses, jotting down notes as thoughts come to you, and as your research spadework digs deeper.

You simply must have notebooks with you day and night. Beside your bed at night, in your bag or pocket by day. With pens that won't run dry at crucial moments of inspiration.

Next - or simultaneously - think your key characters into being. Breathe life into them.

You must appreciate how necessary it is that they should be right in every way for the kind of story you've chosen to write, and for the background, plot and period of your novel.

Your characters may be unusual, or even outrageous by some standards. If they're real to you, you'll be able to make them real to your readers. But don't choose them simply for effect, because you want to shock or write a book that's 'different."

When Barbara Taylor Bradford chose her key character, Emma, for her first successful novel, *'A Woman of Substance'*, she knew she'd got a winner because Emma was her kind of woman. She understood her and could get right into her skin. She could really feel sympathy for her character in everything she did, because author and heroine saw life through the same eyes.

Bear in mind that you and your readers will have to be involved with your key characters for quite a time. So be sure that they're sufficiently interesting to stay the course without boring any of you to tears, or by proving unbelievable.

You must really care what happens to your characters - even if it's a well-deserved bullet at the end of the hard-packed action. Your book doesn't have to end on a happy note - unless it's the kind of story that has led readers to expect one. It just has to ring true.

Read John Steinbeck's novel, *'Of Mice and Men'*, again, and you'll see what I mean. There you have a brilliant example of an action novel with great human and emotional strength. If by any chance you haven't yet read this book, for goodness' sake get it. It will help you enormously.

The bullet that ended the tragic story was inevitable, wasn't it? The compassion behind the killing justified it and was deeply moving.

YOUR PLOT TAKES SHAPE

As your setting and your characters begin to live in your mind, you should find the plot takes shape and begins to fill out. You must have a well constructed plot as well as plenty of action, so this part of your work will take much thought.

Many aspects of the technique used in short story writing and writing a novel are much the same. Although of course there are certain important differences.

For instance, in a novel your plot must cover a far wider range. It must have sufficient incident, enough interest, and relationships, to stay the course for from 60,000 to 80,000, or even up to 150,000 words in some cases.

In the same way, although the dialogue is much the same - it must always ring true to charater, read smoothly, and forward the action or build up the characters or backgrounds. You can be much more expansive in a novel.

It's so satisfying to find, when you're writing a novel, that your characters can take time to explain and express themselves or their actions, than a short story allows. They can grow up, mature, grow old, experience fulfilment or failure, while you're there to control and guide them all the way.

I don't mean for a moment that you may allow the dialogue to run away with you, feeling that you've all the space you can possibly use, and possibly more than you'll know how to fill.

Your dialogue must be saying something. And it must flow naturally - use as little padding as possible. No characters should be allowed to rabbit on. That slows the pace and dulls the interest.

For instance, here's an example of precise English, and of natural dialogue:

A wife is talking to her husband.

'David, I do apologise. I did not go to the airport this morning as you requested because, candidly, I thought it futile.'

Does that ring true? Or does this:

'David, I'm sorry. Really I am. But I didn't go to the airport this morning after all. Oh, I know you asked me to, and I said I would, but honestly Darling, I couldn't see the point after I'd had the 'phone call.'

The first is grammatically correct. But the second is the way people talk - and your characters must talk like ordinary people under all circumstances, if they're to be believable.

SECONDARY CHARACTERS.

You'll readily see that in order to carry the action for the required 70,000 words or so, the two or three key characters will need reinforcements.

This is where your secondary characters and your sub-plots come in.

The secondary character should be as different as possible to the central characters. They should provide relief from the tension of the main plot - or help build it up if it's in danger of sagging.

You can infuse humour, fun, beastliness, saintliness - a little of this goes a long way! - and fine, brave, silly, human virtues through the bit-players in your novel.

But you must exercise complete control over this group or, before you know what's happened, they will have galloped away with the plot, leaving your key characters nursing noses that are badly out of joint, and with nothing interesting to do.

It shouldn't be difficult to build up a colourful company of lesser characters who will appeal to readers in various ways.

After all, almost no one is quite alone in the world. We all have our parents (present or past in the flesh, but whose influence remains forever with us), and very few are without other close relatives, friends, workmates and neighbours. All of whom involve us in their lives to some extent.

Your key characters must be no exception. Their circle of family and friends - or enemies - can afford you the greatest opportunities and satisfaction in the choosing and building up of the interplay of characters, and the weaving of plot and sub-plot.

Shall we see how this can be worked out in actual fact? Here is a break-down of a successful *light romance* which sold well as a book, a serial, and from which a film was made. All of which proves that, whatever you may feel about light romances, the ingredients were right for this particular kind of novel.

BREAKDOWN OF A LIGHT ROMANTIC NOVEL.

It begins, of course, with the central situation.

The heroine has been jilted. Her fiance then has second thoughts and tries to win the girl back. But her faith in him has been shattered, and she finds happiness with someone else - whom we'll call 'the hero', or Second Key Character.

The setting in this case was Switzerland, but it could equally well have been any other colourful place around the world - with which you happen to be familiar - which could provide the necessary hazards and romantic opportunities for the working out of this romance.

If you were writing this novel, having evolved that brief outline, you would concentrate on the characters.

The girl in this particular novel is custom-made for the role she has to play - pretty, attractive, and essentially a happy person, and, when the story opens, she's blissfully anticipating her forthcoming marriage.

Her fiancé is handsome, charming, but weak, and by contrast the other male character - the man who will eventually win the girl - is shown as a rugged type, not necessarily hndsome, but with oodles of charm, and with strength of character.

In this case he was nursing bitterness because of a past unhappy romantic experience, which makes him rather difficult to deal with in the beginning of the story.

Although this is a light romantic novel, these characters must be strongly felt so that they come alive for the reader.

The weak man provides an excellent foil for the strength of the other, and this must be shown in as many ways as possible, but subtly.

(It is quite acceptable for the 'hero' to be confined to a wheel-chair, or to have other physical disabilities, as long as his strength of character and charm overrides it.)

The next step must be to devise details of the action, which will involve the lesser characters whom you must begin to introduce and build up - two-dimentionally, shall we say, rather than three-dimentionally, as are your key characters. Although ALL your characters must hold conviction.

It is largely in the way they affect and expose the lives of your male characters that their importance lies. They must never overshadow them or steal their thunder.

The first chapter sets the tone and pace of the novel. It immediately involves the reader in the lives of the main characters, and draws in the setting.

When the heroine rejects her ex-boyfriend's efforts to heal their relationship - which HE was guilty of breaking - she decides to go to Switzerland to begin a new life, and to be beyond his reach. So she gets a job as a receptionist at an hotel attached to a skiing resort.

Such a setting is perfect for drawing interesting secondary characters into the story, introducing hazards, accidents, love scenes and freaks of weather.

Consider some of the possibities the writer would have at his command...

There could be a lonely chalet where hero and heroine could be snowed up; you could twist his - or her! - ankle, and it would be a simple matter to stage-manage a small avalanche or a blanketing snow-storm. The elements and the setting offer suggestions for drama without end.

In the novel I'm breaking down, the hero was the owner-manager of the hotel. He was abrupt with the girl because she was having to learn her job from scratch and he was under stress. His abruptness to the girl was overheard by an attractive young man, a guest at the hotel, who offered her sympathy.

There you have another secondary character, who could eventually be paired off to another secondary character - a guest, or employee, who has been built up so that her future happiness MATTERS to your readers. Remember, when strings have become too long to be left untied - TIE THEM.

At the crucial moment in the story the weak ex-fiancé turns up at the hotel with the girl he has married for her money, and who already bores him.

Through his arrival misunderstandings arise between the hero and heroine, but of course in the end the right man wins, and the reader, who knew all along that happiness would prevail, is satisfied. The writer hasn't let her down. If she'd wanted to read an upsetting novel that would leave her feeling depressed or let down, she would have chosen another romance, wouldn't she? Or he?

Corny, you say? All right. But I told you how successful it was, didn't I? It must have been what many readers wanted. As the romantic novels of Barbara Cartland and Mills and Boon demonstrate very clearly.

Interest and suspense were maintained through the interplay of the secondary characters who came into the story.

If you were considering writing such a light romantic novel, imagine the possible situations you could introduce.

There could have been a murder at the hotel, or a fire, or a light plane or helicopter could have crashed in a storm with the hero at the controls.

And there would be abundant scope for day to day incidents which would hold the reader's interest... Such as the heroine's first nervous moments on the ski slopes; difficult or humorous hotel guests; a child lost in the snow; and a possible accident involving a cable car.

It would be very helpful if you were familiar with the setting and could write from first hand knowledge, describing the scenery so that you captured your readers' interest - and held it.

Then your finale? How about a masked ball at the hotel or on the lake, which could provide the perfect moment for your two key characters to declare their love - right at the end of the last chapter, not a moment before?

The person who wrote that romantic novel turns out four or five books a year, and her publisher often pays all expenses to cover a working holiday in some romantic or exotic part of the world against which she can write her novels.

But I'm going to tell you a secret... She seems to me to be as bored with her job as any factory worker I've ever met. Churning out these light-weight novels has become a routine job. They're all worked out to very much the same formula, the same length, with the same happy endings.

It may have brought her a great deal of money and a certain fame, but I honestly don't believe it's brought her real fulfilment. As a writer she hasn't expanded her talent with the years; she's remained in one place, ignoring any challenge to try herself out in other fields of work. I think of her as remaining fenced in in a pretty daisy field, queen of her tiny patch of fertile earth, but with all the rest of the world beyond her encircling fence.

If you scoff at the idea of devoting your talent to writing light weight novels exclusively, as this writer does, and you see your work taking its place on the bookstands alongside present writers of Blockbusters, this is what Barbara Taylor Bradford replied when she was asked if she considered her novels - which have made her one of the highest-paid novelists in the world - were 'great literature'?

'I don't think it's great literature, but I do think I'm among the world's best writers of POPULAR literature, if not THE best. I don't mean to sound arrogant, but people really do think my books are wonderful...'. She was only telling the truth. People are avid for her books. Already '*A Woman Of Substance*' has sold more than 12 million copies worldwide. Translated into ten languages, it became the world's fastest selling novel.

And I assure you that this novelist, who wrote her first published book when she was 43 years old, is anything but bored by the kind of books she writes. But then they have considerably more substance than the average light romance. She writes about real people, including herself, and personal experience.

POSSIBLE SUB-PLOTS

Finding sub-plots, and weaving them into your main story can be intriguing and even great fun. And there's really no end to this developments.

When you've worked out your main characters in careful detail and they've come alive for you, and the firm outline of your plot has been constructed; when you've gathered together a lively crowd of secondary characters whom you're anxious to introduce into your novel, then I suggest that you note down some of the possible hazards and distractions that come to mind which could happen in that place and time. Make a list of them so that you can slip them in as you weave your plot more tightly.

You may find them invaluable as you work in greater detail, introducing these highlights strategically so that they can help provide suspense for the curtain that should end each chapter, and get the next one rolling.

There are other reasons why you may find it necessary to introduce these sub-plots. They could lengthen the book if necessary, or they could bring about a change of mood when you find the pace needs speeding up or slowing down.

The sub-plots you weave into your main plot will concern the lives of the secondary characters, and even those who, for one reason or another, have no more than 'walk on' parts to play.

One of the reasons why each chapter should end with a climax in this type of book, is because many light romances or thrillers are serialised in magazines as well as being published in book form, and readers must be left feeling keen to read the next chapter to learn what developments have taken place, what problems resolved.

This technique is very well illustrated in TV and radio serials - best of all in 'soap-operas', such as *'DYNASTY'* and *'DALLAS'*. They're called 'cliff-hangers' as you probably know.

LIGHT ROMANCES UNLIMITED

It's a fact that there's an insatiable public waiting to devour thrillers and light romances without end.

It's also true that they follow a prescribed formula more closely than any other category of novel. If you're drawn to this kind of writing, study some of the stream of such books published by Mills and Boon, for instance, although there are, of course, other publishers who specialise in such books.

Certain publishers specialise in hardback as well as in paperback editions of light romances, while others bring out paperbacks exclusively.

I must warn you that you will be wasting your time if you try to write them without first making a thorough study of these novels. They're far more difficult than they may appear to be.

If you can master the formula of one or other of the publishers of these light romances or thrillers, and you're 'taken on' as they say, it will probably mean that you'll be expected to write from two to five a year. From now to doomsday. And very nice too, if that's the kind of fiction you want to write, AND CAN WRITE, and if money is of first importance.

The terms are very good with some of these publishers, bad with others, so choose carefully. Never, under any circumstances, part with your copyright. No matter what kind of fiction you write, always sell on a royalty agreement.

This means that you should receive an advance against royalties when you sign the agreement, possibly another advance on publication, and then royalties paid yearly or half-yearly, from which the advance payments will naturally be deducted.

If you part with your copyright you will receive no further benefit from your book, whether it sells a paperback edition in addition to the hardback, foreign rights, serial rights, digest rights, television, radio or film rights. The small print of Agreements must be studied very carefully indeed.

THE REWARDS OF CRIME

Crime fiction has an enormous following the world over, and in Britain we can be proud of having some of the finest in the world. Past and present.

Strangely enough, women writers seem drawn to crime writing even more than men. Agatha Christie and Dorothy Sayers set the ball rolling, and it's been gathering momentum ever since.

Ruth Rendell is often bracketed with P.D. James as the present 'Queen of Crime', but she doesn't confine her writing to this category, and many prefer to call her one of the best novelists writing in Britain today.

As Moira Paterson wrote in a recent interview which she had persuaded Ruth Rendell to give her:

'Since her first book, *'From Doon With Death'* in 1964, her 25 novels and four collections of short stories have extended crime fiction far beyond the boundaries of intricate puzzles elegantly solved. She has won many awards - The Crime Writers' Association Gold and Silver Daggers, two Mystery Writers of America Edgar Awards and the Arts Council National Book Award - and an enormous readership worldwide. Her books are translated into 16 languages.

'Ruth Rendell writes two kinds of fiction. Her detective novels, set in the imaginary country town of Kingsmarkham, feature Chief Inspector Reg Wexford and his assistant, Inspector Mike Burden.'

So far there have been 13 Wexford books, with more to follow.

'In her non-Wexford novels the identity of the criminal is usually revealed early on,' Moira Paterson tells us. 'The mystery lies in what makes these people 'instruments of disaster.' The setting is hauntingly realised. Faced with ruin, her characters tug their threadbare skirts of respectability over their knees.'

Ruth Rendell reveals, 'Chance intersts me very much, in life as in fiction. I like to reflect on the relative weight of determination and accident. Sometimes I think that just one step, say to the left instead of the right, can cause a whole chain of change.'

Twenty-nine books in 21 years is an impressive output, and very soon sees the appearance of her first novel under a different name - *' A Dark Adapted Eye'* by Barbara Vine. Although this new book does contain murder and mystery, by no stretch of the term can it be called 'crime fiction.' Her own background and memories of the immediately post-war world are reflected in the book.

'But every character a writer creates is very much him or herself,' she insists. She isn't trying to hide behind the use of a pseudonym. 'I just wanted a new name because I'm using a different voice,' she explains.

Ruth Rendell dispels readers' fears that she may be 'writing herself out.'

'I have quite enough material to keep two novelists going,' she says. 'I'm a compulsive writer. Possibly I'm afraid that if I don't keep on doing it I won't be able to do it any more.

LITERARY AGENTS.

This is where the services of a reliable Literary Agent could well come in.

When we were studying the marketing of Short Stories or Features, I said that it was unrealistic to expect an Agent to handle the selling of such work before you had built up a reputation, and proved that your work was saleable. A writer's work must be known and in some demand before an Agent will show interest.

With novels the situation is different.

Most first novels are handled by the author, unless they have outstanding promise. Then an Agent may be prepared to act on the author's behalf from book one.

Or an Agent may take over and conclude a transaction when a publisher has accepted a first novel, or shown some definite interest in it. Then the Agent may relieve the author of the considerable responsiblity involved in the sale of a book.

There's a very great deal more to exchanging contracts between author and publisher than the signing of signatures.

The legal implications implicit in the small print of a contract demand a certain amount of legal know-how, and fortunes have certainly been lost by authors through ignorance or carelessness.

The ways in which an author can be protected and helped by the services of a good literary agent are manifold. I suggest that you study the section in your copy of '*The Writers And Artists'*

Year Book' devoted to Copywright and Literary Agents, for enlightenment.

Not only will an author be protected from signing away his copyright and sacrificing his royalties, but a reliable Agent will shepherd him through possible future transactions, and build up connections with publishers.

Such an Agent will be familiar with markets and demands, and the publishers to be approached will in all probability be known to him, at least by reputation.

To illustrate the kind of disaster that can befall an author who sells a book without such protection and guidance, let me tell you what happened to Graham Greene early in his writing career. It has only recently come to light, and has a lesson writers would do well to study - and remember.

A SALUTARY LESSON.

Forty years ago Graham Greene was a struggling novelist in middle age who, despite having already written some of his best work, hasn't achieved the sort of recognition which made him confident of being able to support his wife and family after the war.

Rather than write pot-boilers or journalism to earn a living until such time as his serious novels paid the way, Graham Greene sold his services to Metro Goldwyn Mayer Films, and in the course of two years on their payroll he wrote, among other work, a short novel designed to be made into a film. It was called *'The Tenth Man'* .

Entering into this agreement direct with MGM, without the guidance of an Agent, Graham Greene exchanged all rights to the novel for the salary he received as a member of the writing staff.

Perhaps for that reason, the author forgot all about this novel over the busy years, and was surprised to hear of its existence again in 1983 when he was told that MGM had sold it for an enormous sum to the British publisher, Anthony Blond.

Inevitably it has become a best-seller and will undoubtedly make a fortune - for others. Graham Greene won't get a cent of it. He signed away all his rights in it way back in 1937!

Very fortunately this author doesn't actually need the royalties *'The Tenth Man'* has earned and will continue to earn. But it could have been otherwise, and in any case it hardly seems fair, does it?

Since those hard years when Graham Greene was trying to make a name for himself as an author, and at times finding the going very tough indeed, his business affairs have naturally been taken over by a Literary Agent, and he has been able to devote himself to the demanding work of writing excellent novels, all of them bestsellers of course.

THIS TIP MAY HELP YOU.

When writing HISTORICAL NOVELS I strongly recommend this plan of action...

The best way to work yourself into the mood, the period, and the skins of your characters, is to write short stories and articles on the subject. It will build up your pace and confidence in the job-in-hand, and help you to master your subject in all its complexity.

This was the method used by Irving Stone when he was working on those monumental biographical novels of his - Vincent van Gogh's life story in *'Lust For Life'*, Jack London's in *'Sailor On Horseback'* 'and *'The Agony And The Ecstasy'* which brillliantly tells of the life and work of Michaelangelo.

Through the seven years that he was writing his book about Michaelangelo, he was turning out a stream of articles about the man, his work, and his times, which were published and acclaimed all over the world.

This was most important in a number of ways:

1. It was limbering Irving Stone up for the great task in hand.

2. It was helping him to clarify the various aspects of characterisation as well as the background, by writing these short pieces, most of which were later embodied in the book.

3. And it was also awakening a world-wide interest in his subject, so that, when his novel was eventually published, readers were conditioned and eager to receive it. They had learnt many fascinating facts about the genius, and they were avid to know much more.

Even after the great book was published, and believe me it was a blockbuster in every way, Irving Stone continued to write articles about Michelangelo, for he had gathered so much material that couldn't be included in the novel, and couldn't bear to see it 'wasted.' Also, he hadn't completely worked himself out of the skin of his beloved character, and he had to set himself free.

There's another sound reason for working on these lines, although it didn't apply to Irving Stone.

A writer must live. He must cope with the wolf without so that he doesn't become the wolf within. And it takes a long time before one can expect to reap financial benefits from a book - unless one is established as an author, or has written a most unusually promising best-seller, when some publishers will pay substantial sums in advance royalties before the book is an established fact.

So the flow of articles and short stories could very well go on while a writer is engaged on producing his book, unless he has other sources of income to tide him over the lean period. After all, it's easier than becoming a postman or a typist over the working-waiting period I would say.

Irving Stone left us with this gem of wisdom to think about:

'FEAR OF FAILURE HAS PREVENTED MORE PEOPLE FROM WRITING THAN I CAN SAY.' He knew, if anyone did, that it takes courage and much hard work to become a good, successful writer.

ACTION NOVELS.

It's essential, of course, that an Action Novel shall have a tightly woven plot, that padding is kept to a minimum since its slows action down, and that the characters shall be sufficiently dynamic and interesting to hold the attention and concern of the reader from first to last.

There are, of course, many kinds of action novel . You'll find action galore in Wilbur Smith's novels, as there is in those of Frederick Forsyth, Hammond Innis, and many many more good writers in this genre.

And it's easy to see why such books readily sell their serial rights to magazines and digests, as well as their foreign, radio, and probably their film and small-screen rights as well.

Few types of novel sell as well or as widely as the thriller. And I've been intrigued to observe how often thriller-writers have sound business sense. They - and their agents - seem to handle their affairs most efficiently, and to get a gret kick out of this side of writing.

Once again I cite Jeffrey Archer, because he's so brilliantly capable of getting the most out of his work, from choosing his subject for its immediacy and topical impact, to promoting the end product to the world in every possible way, and obviously enjoying the whole shebang enormously.

Don't be so foolish as to let envy convince you that these great success stories are the flukes of luck. They're nothing of the kind, as every experienced writer knows only too well.

There must be meticulous timing, planning and attention to detail; there must be considerable research and self-discipline for even the most naturally gifted authors to win their glittering prizes.

Quite apart from the sheer hard work involved, and the sacrifices of fun, family life, and the company of friends to a large extent, just imagine having to take on the load of promotional work when at last your book is an accomplished fact, and it has appeared between covers.

When this happens, all most authors want to do is to close the door and go off somewhere with their nearest and dearest, or alone, to relax in the sun and gather their exhausted mental and physical resources together again.

But they can't, can they? Usually, if the book's anything of a success, there are the receptions and parties. There are the endless interviews set up for the press, radio and screen. There are the copies of their book to sign in shops and at book fairs. Authors have to be seen looking the way the public expects to see them. I can imagine this taking considerable effort.

Of course there are those authors who simply bask in all the publicity. Who declare that it's great fun, and who enjoy giving themselves and their wardrobes a new look for the occasion.

But to very many authors, the promotion at the end of the game is the hardest work of all.

Think of that when you envy them their rewards of toil and dedication! It's quite a thought.

* * * * *

If you doubt your talent - and we all do at times - bear in mind what Henry Miller wrote for you to think about:

'EVERYONE HAS TALENT AND, WITH CULTIVATION, COULD PRODUCE SOMETHING. THERE SHOULD BE FIRE, PASSION, AN OBSESSIVE URGE. ONE SHOULD NOT BE CONCERNED WHETHER A BOOK TURNS OUT GOOD OR BAD, ONE SHOULD WRITE, WRITE, AND THINK OF NOTHING ELSE. I CANNOT URGE YOU TOO OFTEN - WRITE. WRITE. WRITE...'

There could be no better advice than this.

And now, all success to you! And succeed you will - if you keep faith and write something every day. You have my word for it, my friend!

The Malvern Publishing Company Limited

Trading patterns and business practices in the publishing industry have combined to create a situation where publication of a first novel has become very difficult. This is no reflection on the wealth of new talent that abounds but rather an indictment of the system. The Malvern Publishing Company Limited was founded in May 1984 in an attempt to fill this gap by producing a list composed entirely of first novels.

The Management of the Company have gained their experience in publishing as Literary Agents and, as such, feel they are well qualified to recognise talented work and guage its value. Our list is modest but we will be adding to it regularly.

The first six titles all used the distinctive FIRST NOVEL logo on their jackets. During 1985, we changed to using illustrated jackets, the first title using this format was A HEAD ON MY SHOULDERS by Vesper Hunter. The MPC logo is used for our non-fiction titles and second novels.

Our 1986 list consists of twenty new titles, some of which are the second and third books by our original authors. However, most are new authors thus continuing our policy of giving new writers opportunities to get into print and for you, the reader, to enjoy their work.

WE ARE NOT VANITY OR SUBSIDY PUBLISHERS

CEDAR by James Murphy
ISBN 0-947993-22-3
An outstanding, up to the minute, spy thriller about international espionage and the nuclear disarmament problem. A *must* for spy story fans.

CHANEY'S CHOICE by Chris Parker
ISBN 0-947993-26-6
A thriller of a different kind, but just as riveting, about a television show host who goes all out to destroy those whom he interviews. It will keep you awake at night!

These titles can be obtained from most good bookshops or direct from::

Malvern Publishing Company Limited, P.O. Box 16, Malvern, Worcestershire WR14 1UH.